The Art of Touch

the art

Edited by

Joan Schweighardt

Faye Rapoport DesPres

# of touch

A Collection of
Prose and Poetry
from the Pandemic
and Beyond

The University of Georgia Press

Athens

The editors acknowledge the previous publication of the following materials:
Erika Dreifus, "Miriam, Quarantined," previously published on the 929 website
and in *Birthright: Poems* by Erika Dreifus (Kelsay Books). Daniel B. Summerhill,
"Considering the Defence Production Act," first appeared in *Split This Rock*.
Laura Crucianelli, "The Need to Touch," first appeared in *Aeon*. Quintin Collins,
"Bridge Strike on Storrow Drive," used with the permission of The Ohio State
University. Anne Casey, "Vestigial Imprint," from Anne Casey, *Portrait of a Woman
Walking Home* (Canerra: Recent Work Press, 2021). Selection from Anne Marie
Oomen, *As Long as I Know You* (Athens: University of Georgia Press, 2022),
copyright 2022 The University of Georgia Press. Susan J. Tweit, "Regaining Touch
with Our Humanity," first published in *Colorado Central Magazine*.

Designed by Kaelin Chappell Broaddus
Set in 9.8/13.5 Dolly Pro Regular by Kaelin Chappell Broaddus

Most University of Georgia Press titles are
available from popular e-book vendors.

Printed digitally

Library of Congress Cataloging-in-Publication Data
Names: Schweighardt, Joan, editor. | DesPres, Faye Rapoport, 1962– editor.
Title: The art of touch : a collection of prose and poetry from the pandemic and beyond /
    edited by Joan Schweighardt, Faye Rapoport DesPres.
Description: Athens : The University of Georgia Press, 2023.
Identifiers: LCCN 2023017135 | ISBN 9780820365336 (paperback) | ISBN 9780820365343
    (epub) | ISBN 9780820365350 (pdf)
Subjects: LCSH: Touch—Literary collections. | LCGFT: Literature.
Classification: LCC PN6071.T68 A78 2023 | DDC 808.8—dc23/eng/20230615
LC record available at https://lccn.loc.gov/2023017135

Contents

Touch Redux

Acknowledgments

The Art of Touch has been a true literary adventure for us—sometimes overwhelming, often inspiring, and ultimately rewarding. We are so grateful to Bethany Sneed, acquisitions editor at UGA Press, for seeing the potential in our project and for her ongoing patience as she led us through the production process. We are also grateful to Elizabeth Adams, assistant to the director and rights and permissions coordinator/ intellectual property manager at UGA Press, for illuminating our path through what might otherwise have seemed a dark forest of contracts, permission reprint requests, and other official procedures. We appreciate the hard work of each staff person at the University of Georgia Press who worked on this book. The expertise of project editor Jon Davies and copy editor Ivo Fravashi were invaluable to us.

We would never have begun this journey if not for Elizabeth Trupin-Pulli. We are thankful for her warmth, wisdom, and guidance and for helping us get *The Art of Touch* on its feet.

Last but never least, we must thank our contributors—not only for their wonderful work but also for their enthusiasm, patience, and support all through this process.

Thank you.

The Art of Touch

Introduction

JOAN SCHWEIGHARDT

I began thinking about touch when my sister died in 2017. Judy, who was ten years younger than me, liked me to swing her in circles when she was a toddler, but as she grew older, she made it clear that she disdained most forms of physical contact, particularly from me—and possibly related to her diagnosis of schizophrenia. I can't remember ever hugging her, and I know she never hugged me. Hence, I sat at her bedside—in the hospital and later in hospice—for ten days straight, until the end, and never once touched her.

She was unconscious the whole time, so I could have touched her arm or placed a finger alongside her cheek; certainly, the caregivers who came and went did so. But the caregivers didn't know her. I felt I couldn't risk that she would sense my touch among all the others and fume inwardly because I, who knew the rules, had broken them. Instead, I read her Jennifer Egan's *Manhattan Beach* from beginning to end, in the hope that she would recognize my voice and know I was there—and at a safe distance.

At about the same time I lost Judy, Linda (whose story is included in these pages) lost her sister Lois to multiple system atrophy (MSA). Every Friday, for the nearly two years it took for Lois's muscles to atrophy to the point where she could no longer do anything for herself, including communicate, Linda went to Lois's house and washed and styled her hair, gave her a manicure, pedicure, facial massage, hugs, kisses, the works. Linda is very good at touching people—she does it for a living; she is an electrologist (with licenses in hair styling and dental hygiene) as well as a writer!—and Lois, who had been a hair stylist herself, knew how to receive touch.

The difference between the ways in which Linda and I said goodbye to our dying sisters got me thinking about the difference between people who touch and people who aren't all that good at it. I belong somewhere in the latter category, I suppose, though not anywhere near the bottom. Until my sister lay on her deathbed, her reluctance to be touched had not really been an issue for me—but not so much because of where I sit on the bell curve. One of the many characteristics she exhibited was a total disregard for basic hygiene. She grew up oblivious to germs, and I grew up apprehensive about them.

And so I pondered. Stereotypically speaking, the French kiss even casual acquaintances on both cheeks; the Japanese prefer bows. When my son brought his Korean fiancée to the house for the first time, I threw the door wide open and enfolded her in my arms. They'd dated for several months when he was stationed in South Korea; I'd heard so much about her by the time she arrived in the United States that I'd fallen in love with her myself. Later, when she was fluent enough in English to reminisce with me, she said I nearly scared her to death hugging her like that; people didn't greet people that way in her country, especially at initial introductions. Seeing myself from her perspective, I imagined a raptor swooping down to envelop its prey.

I started talking about touch to friends who are writers, psychologists, massage therapists, and healthcare workers. What I discovered is that everyone has something thought-provoking to say about the importance of touch, or the ramifications of its absence. Many people are, like me, concerned that technology makes it too easy to break the habit of touching our loved ones. Some feel that touch need not be restricted to the physical realm at all, that you can touch a person with words, through literature, through performance. People shared their stories. One woman said she had found it hard to touch her mother, who was in a nursing home and had been diagnosed with, among other things, dementia. But when her aging dog got sick, she found herself on the floor each evening after work, massaging him to ease his pain. After the dog's passing, she was able to take this skill to the nursing home and begin to massage her mother in her last days.

And then, in 2020, the coronavirus threatened the planet, and the issue of whether to touch or not touch rose to a whole new level of concern.

A year after the virus struck, a friend of a friend who I hoped to know better in the future told me in an email that I was the last person to hug her. At the very beginning of the quarantine, I had taken her to the hospital for a colonoscopy—because her best friend was out of town, and I was close by and working from home. I sat in the car that day to avoid the people in the waiting room. Twice I had to go in anyway to use the bathroom. I carried disinfectant wipes, and I employed them to touch the doorknob, toilet handle, and sink faucet. I had to enter the hospital once again to retrieve her, and then I drove her home and walked her into her house because she was still groggy. I was in a hurry to leave because I was worried about germs and had been all day. But before I left, I gave her a half-hearted hug, because we'd been on a journey together: she'd had a colonoscopy, always a scary proposition, and I'd been dodging germs— real or imagined—in order to honor a commitment I'd made back before the virus really got going.

I was shocked to learn that the anemic hug she'd received from me—a woman who is not a great hugger to begin with—was the last one she'd had for a solid year. My first thought was, *She deserved better!* My second was, *Giving someone a hug is an awesome responsibility!*

I asked people I knew who lived alone if they remembered who hugged them last before the pandemic, and, to my surprise, they always did, right down to the where and when. Moreover, they were eager to describe the hug itself—how long it lasted, how genuine it felt—and the circumstances in which it took place. The last two people to hug my friend Alice before the vaccine were a married couple she'd gone to dinner with. The numbers were just beginning to climb then where she lives in New York City, and she went into quarantine that very same week. But the couple she'd dined with waited an additional week, to have a few more meals out with a few more friends before holing up in their apartment—and they both got COVID. The husband died, alone, in the hospital, after weeks on a ventilator. His wife recovered.

Touching, so many of us have come to realize, is complicated. Maybe as she lay in her transitional state, hovering someplace between life and death, my sister would have welcomed a hug, even from me—maybe especially from me—and I have come to regret I didn't give her one. On the other hand, maybe it wouldn't have mattered to her one way or the other. I will never know. I can only tell you that I have been on a cerebral journey through the jungle of touch ever since her passing, and when Faye Rapoport DesPres, my dear friend and colleague of many years, joined me on this trail, *The Art of Touch* had its inception.

In these pages we offer you a sweeping compilation of many ways to think about touch, or the lack thereof, during pandemic times as well as generally. In *Touch Is Joy*, you will find joy in abundance, the joy of living in worlds—real and imagined—where touch is ongoing, pandemic or otherwise. *Touch Is Science* features a powerful essay by a neuroscientist on how "the language of touch binds our minds and bodies to the broader social world." In *Touch Is Healing*, a deep tissue massage therapist describes the emotional impact that often accompanies the physical during treatments, while the therapist/lecturer who created Verbal First Aid™ describes how her program, used by first responders worldwide, heals people who can't always be touched. In *The Sanctity of Touch*, authors reflect on the memory of touch, while in *Touch Is Not Always Human*, we learn how one writer came to develop a fluency in Equus while another tells the sweet story of the day his partner's dog finally kissed him. In *Touch: A Broader Perspective*, we honor the magic of being able to be "in touch," how audiences can be stirred through words, through performance; and why students who are blind often prefer instructions focused on their uniquely attuned fingertips to their instructor's physical adjustments. *Touch Delayed* reflects on the loss of the chance to touch. *Tumultuous Touch* reminds us that touch can be traumatic, as a massage experience awakens memories of stark brutality in one piece, and a mother (and mental health counselor) shares the challenges she faces along with her child, who lives with OCD, in another. We end our collection with hope, in a section called *Touch Redux*.

Although no anthology can expect to cover the complete range of voices that have something to say on any one subject, we strove to include as many unique voices here as possible. Our hope is that you will find this work to be a kind of embrace in itself.

touch is joy

Joicing

JOY CASTRO

In Heaven I watch Jennifer Lopez pole-dance all day but sun-drunk in a field of poppies. In Heaven I eat my grandmother's garlic roast pork & sweet gold platanos all day & never grow full, but no real pig, kind & intelligent, felt fear & died, & no real people worked far too hard for too little. In Heaven my man makes me come with his mouth & hands, &c., all night & I never grow tired, but we never veer around each other in our large apartment that suddenly, months ago, grew too small, & I never bristle & brace at things he says, & likewise. In Heaven I hug my grown son tight, rejoicing with gold light I've known since he grew real, & there's no pane of glass between us, the glimmering ghost of my own reflection distracting me & muffling my view of him.

As is so often the case, with people.

Why is there only *rejoicing*, never joicing for the first time, when everything is new? Must all love be laced with the taste of saudade? Refuse.

In the future, if I die right now of plague, archaeologists can dig up my bones & know that I was fifty-two & tallish, that I'd borne a child, broken a leg, suffered each day with a twisted spine I hid. They could speculate while hefting the rack of my ribs. When is a cradle not a cage? But they couldn't feel the way this fist of meat still throbs: giant heart, brave heart, lion heart, Arabian-horse heart, fleet & fearless, at the center of my everything, even now, even amidst all this.

Touching the Nooks and Crannies of My Soul

GRACE ANNE STEVENS

I have led many different lives.

I remember each of them, being astonished by them all, and at long last I am able to look back at how much I have changed and learned throughout this journey. My broad smile appears not only on my face but also within my soul.

Just to keep it simple, along the way, I changed marital status from single to married and raising a family with three children to divorced. I have changed careers from engineering to counselling to speaking and writing. And, perhaps less common, I changed gender from male to female at the age of sixty-four.

It is this last change, which began about a decade ago, that also intensified my understanding of the many meanings of *touch*. In January 2010 I began the process of swapping the hormones that would be flowing through my bloodstream by suppressing natural testosterone and adding estrogen to my system. I formally transitioned my gender visibly to the world fifteen months later. I have been one of the lucky ones; I have not lost any of my family as a result of my decision to live my truth.

I had heard from others who had taken similar journeys that estrogen could calm you down and soften your skin, though at that time I couldn't imagine what that might mean. Now, after ten years on E, I have a better feel for it. In fact, I have a better feel for just about everything that goes on around me and within me. Most of the time the impact of E has been a pleasant and welcomed surprise, the counterpart to the shock of realizing what I was missing for most of my life.

———

I suspect that most of us, whether we admit it or not, have struggled to understand what makes us us. For so many years of my journey I could not make sense of how to align the conflicts among my mind, body, and spirit, each seemingly represented by different voices within me not only telling me different things but hardly ever agreeing on who I was. Looking back, I realize that all of these battles were how I experienced my own gender dysphoria. For me the primary result was expressed by my inability to feel on each of the competing levels. This meant I often became numb to physical and emotional touch. If I allowed the magic of touch to be processed, I would have to deal with the lack of alignment my entire system was unwilling to face.

"The soul is the truth of who we are, the light, the love that is within us. It goes by different names, but it is the truth of us." —Marianne Williamson

I was living in a darkness that I was unaware of. I could not understand the concept of love, either for myself or for others. I acted as if I could, and fooled most of the world, including my family, and all too often myself.

I regard the path I began in 2009 as leaping off a cliff with no parachute and no idea where the ground was. Now, a decade later, my mind, body, and spirit have not only aligned but have worked through the multitudes of psychological and "authenticity" battles that have occurred. In each moment mind, body, and spirit are willing, alone and together, to let the touch of each new feeling in, to be explored without judgment, without fear, and with love. I am, at long last, happily exploring the nooks and crannies of my soul.

My sense is this would never have been possible without what I lovingly refer to as my drug of choice, my daily intake of estrogen. It is not the engineer in me; I cannot put a metric on it that tries to evaluate its reach. Perhaps it is the holistic counselor in me that recognizes that the whole (of me) is greater than the sum of my parts. I do have the sense that the softness E has provided to my skin is one part of an immeasurable softness I experience in the rest of me. In spite of the apparent easiness of getting black and blue from the gentlest of bumps, which many women experience, I would not willingly want to let go of the ability to feel all that I can and do now.

I no longer step away from a touch, a handshake, a hug as I did for so long, and I let the energy from these contacts linger as they travel through my system. I can thoroughly enjoy the unintended kick that may startle me in the middle of night when sharing my bed, as I never did when I was married. I am working hard in balancing the loss of some of this due to the present pandemic, yet I revel in the joy that now, in living my truth, I have the ability to feel these touches, inside and out, and dream of the day when human contact and connection can safely return. Speaking of dreaming, I like to borrow and paraphrase from *Hamlet*: To be true, or not to be true, To touch, perchance to feel. For in that touch of life, your dreams come true.

Being true to myself has always been my lifelong dream, and for the last decade I have been living it and have learned that it is an ongoing journey of exploration with love and no regrets. The journey became easier once I learned to touch myself and others with my mind, body, and spirit, even if I needed a little hormonal support to achieve it.

Each of our journeys is unique, and there are an infinity of paths that can be followed. I consider myself blessed to have found my path of truth and authenticity, and wish you the best in seeking out and finding yours.

Tactile Ghazal

ALISON STONE

Locked down with family, I'm blessed with touch.
For some autistics, pets give the best touch.

The blind, bony cat still snuggles and purrs.
Mind ruined, my grandfather regressed, touch

the only language he still understood.
The daycare worker craves a rest from touch.

One ivy vine spread to swallow the hedges.
Glances and flirty words progressed to touch.

When the veteran trembles, his wife knows—lift
his shirt. Her hands warm, each scar caressed—touch

brings him home. A hand-squeeze, a hug, a back
massage comfort. But—slap, shove, grabbed breast—touch

also brings infinite shades of pain. K
was never exposed, never confessed. Touch

he may have long-forgotten marks her still.
Close-up of the actress's large chest: *Touch-*

a toucha half-dressed Janet sings.
Frankie's creature acts at her behest—*Touch*

me. In lucky beds, lips fat from kissing,
crotches sore, red marks where fingers pressed—touch-

satiated lovers drift into dream.
Posed in a boat in winter, hair messed, touch

of blush, the model pretends the camera
is a hand. Lets herself be undressed. *Touch*

someone, urges the phone company ad.
Given a chance, the nerd impressed with touch.

Pre-Covid, my daughter approached each dog
she saw, would cross the street to request touch.

Gulls squabble over scraps while noon sun burns
unwary worshipers. Waves swell, crest, touch

the shoreline only as they peter out
In latex gloves, the doctor's dressed for touch.

Praise, Stone, the lonely souls who don't give up,
who haunt bars and parks in a quest for touch.

touch is science

The Need to Touch

The Language of Touch Binds Our Minds and Bodies to the Broader Social World. What Happens When Touch Becomes Taboo?

LAURA CRUCIANELLI

Touch is the first sense by which we encounter the world and the final one to leave us as we approach death's edge. "Touch comes before sight, before speech," writes Margaret Atwood in her novel *The Blind Assassin* (2000). "It is the first language and the last, and it always tells the truth." Our biology bears this out. Human foetuses are covered in fine hairs known as lanugo, which appear around sixteen weeks of pregnancy. Some researchers believe that these delicate filaments enhance the pleasant sensations of our mother's amniotic fluid gently washing over our skin, a precursor to the warm and calming feeling that a child, once born, will derive from being hugged.

Touch has always been my favourite sense—a loyal friend, something I can rely on to lift me up when I'm feeling down or spread joy when I'm on a high. As an Italian living abroad for more than a decade, I often suffered from a kind of touch hunger, which had knock-on consequences for my mood and health more generally. People in northern Europe use social touch much less than people in southern Europe. In hindsight, it's not surprising that I spent the past few years studying touch as a scientist.

Lately, though, touch has been going through a "prohibition era": it's been a rough time for this most important of the senses. The 2020 pandemic served to make touch the ultimate taboo, next to coughing and sneezing in public. While people suffering from COVID-19 can lose the sense of smell and taste, touch is the sense that has been diminished for almost all of us, test-positive or not, symptomatic or not, hospitalised or not. Touch is the sense that has paid the highest price.

But if physical distance is what protects us, it's also what stands in the way of care and nurturance. Looking after another human being almost inevitably involves touching them—from the very basic needs of bathing, dressing, lifting, assisting, and medical treatment (usually referred to as *instrumental* touch) to the more affective tactile exchanges that aim to communicate, provide comfort, and offer support (defined as *expressive* touch). Research in osteopathy and manual therapy, where practitioners have been working closely with neuroscientists on affective touch, suggests[1] that the beneficial effect of massage therapy goes well beyond the actual manoeuvre performed by the therapist. Rather, there is something special simply in the act of resting one's hands on the skin of the client. There is no care, there is no cure, without touch.

The present touch drought arrived after a period in which people were already growing more afraid of touching one another. Technology has enabled this distance, as social networking sites have become the primary source of social interaction for children and adolescents. A recent survey showed[2] that 95 per cent of teens have access to a smartphone, and 45 per cent say that they are online "almost constantly."

Another reason for touch-scepticism is the growing global awareness of how touch is a weapon that men use to impose their power over women. The #MeToo movement exposed how women are expected to acquiesce to inappropriate touch as the cost of gaining access to certain kinds of opportunities. Meanwhile, doctors, nurses, teachers, and salespeople are all guided against being too "hands-on." Yet studies suggest that touch actually improves the quality of our encounters with any of these professionals and makes us evaluate the experience more positively. For example,[3] we are likely to give a more generous tip to a waiter who absently touches our shoulder when taking the order than to those who keep their distance.

What's unique about touch, when set against the other senses, is its mutuality. While we can look without being looked back at, we can't touch without being touched in return. During the pandemic, nurses and doctors have talked about how this unique characteristic of touch helped them communicate with patients. When they couldn't talk, smile, or be seen properly because of their protective equipment, medical professionals could always rely on a pat on the shoulder, holding a hand, or squeezing an arm to reassure patients and let them know that they were not alone. In a pandemic where touch is a proven vector, paradoxically it's also a part of the cure. Touch really is the ultimate tool for social connection, and the good news is that we were born fully accessorised to make the most of it.

In the 1990s, there was a wave of research demonstrating the shocking consequences of touch deprivation on human development. Several studies showed[4] that children from Romanian orphanages who were barely touched in the first years of life had cognitive and behavioural deficits later on, as well as significant differences in brain development. In adulthood, people with reduced social contact have a higher[5] risk of dying earlier compared with people with strong social relationships. Touch is especially important as we age: for instance, gentle touch has been shown[6] to increase the amount of food intake in a group of institutionalised elderly adults. Even when we can't see, hear, or speak as we used to, we can almost always rely on touch to explore the world around us, to communicate with others, and to allow them to communicate with us.

Science is now beginning to provide an account of why touch matters so much. Touch on the skin can reduce heartrate, blood pressure, and cortisol levels—all factors related to stress—in both adults and babies. It facilitates[7] the release of oxytocin, a hormone that provides sensations of calm, relaxation, and being at peace with the world. Every time we hug a friend or snuggle a pet, oxytocin is released in our body, giving us that feel-good sensation. In this way, oxytocin appears to reinforce our motivation to seek and maintain contact with others, which assists in the development of humans' socially oriented brains. Oxytocin also plays a vital role in the relationship we have with ourselves.

In our lab, we recently showed that oxytocin might promote processes of multisensory integration, the so called "glue of the senses"—the way the world typically presents itself to us as a coherent picture, rather than as multiple distinct streams of sense data. Multisensory integration, in turn, is at the root of our sense of body ownership, the feeling that most take for granted, that our body is *ours*. For our studies, we invited people to the lab, and induced the rubber hand illusion, a well-established set-up where participants look at a lifelike rubber hand being touched while their own hand, hidden out of view, is touched at the same time. After a minute or so of synchronous tactile stimulation, the vast majority of participants experience the illusion that the rubber hand *is* their own hand, that they embody the rubber hand. We found that applying the tactile stimulation at slow, caress-like velocities enhances the illusion of embodying the rubber hand. Furthermore, we also found[8] that giving participants one dose of intranasal oxytocin before the illusion enhanced the experience, compared with a placebo. In other words, affective touch and oxytocin might boost the process that keeps us grounded to a physical body.

Touch is the first sense to develop, and is mediated by the skin, our largest organ. We are one of the few mammals to be born so premature in the trajectory of our development. Our motor system isn't fully developed, we can't feed ourselves, we can't regulate our own temperature beyond a certain threshold—all of which means that we rely on others to survive. As a child, being cared for depends primarily on tactile contact and "being held." Any basic activity involves touch, such as changing nappies, having a bath, being fed, sleeping, and, of course, cuddling. Even after we make it through the first few months of life, social tactile interactions are crucial[9] for our development. For example, postnatal depression is known to have negative consequences for infants, but maternal touch can also have a protective effect. So, encouraging tactile interactions between mothers with depression and their babies can reduce negative outcomes for the children later on in life. Importantly, the benefit is reciprocal: skin-to-skin contact between infant and parent increases the levels of oxytocin in mothers, fathers, and infants, providing a feel-good sensation, promoting the development of a healthy relationship, and enhancing synchrony in parent-infant interactions.

Slow, caress-like touch was more likely to communicate love, even when delivered by a stranger.

Many neuroscientists and psychologists believe[10] that we have a dedicated system just for the perception of social—affective—touch distinct from the one that we use to touch objects. This system seems to be able to selectively recognise caress-like touch; this is then processed in the insula, a brain area connected to maintaining our sense of self and an awareness of our body. Slow, caress-like touch is not only important for our survival but also for our cognitive and social development: for example, it can influence the way we learn to identify and recognise other people from early in life. In a study[11] of four-month-old infants, when parents provided gentle stroking, children were able to learn to identify a previously seen face better than those who experienced nontactile stimulation. It seems that slow, social touch might act as a cue to pay particular attention to social stimuli, such as faces.

What's particularly important in infancy and childhood is not only the amount of touch we receive but also its nature and quality. In a recent study,[12] my colleagues and I showed that infants as young as twelve months are able to detect the way that their mothers touch them during daily activities, such as during play time or while sharing a book together. In our study, the mothers didn't know that we were interested in touch, which allowed us to have a real insight into their spontaneous interactions. Importantly, we found that mothers' ability to understand their infants' needs translated into a kind of tactile language: for example, those mothers who were less aligned or responsive to their babies also tended to use more rough and restrictive touch. Infants also tended to reciprocate, in that they were more likely to use aggressive touch towards their mothers if this was the way that they were touched.

It's not an exaggeration to talk of touch as a kind of language—one that we learn, like spoken language, through social interactions with our loved ones, from the earliest stages of our life. We use touch every day to communicate our emotions, and to tell someone that we are scared, happy, in love, sad, sexually aroused, and much more. In turn, we are pretty good at reading other people's intentions and emotions based on the way that they touch us. In a recent study,[13] we invited people to the lab and asked them to detect the emotions and intentions that the experimenter was trying to convey to them via touch. The touch was delivered at different velocities: slower, as the touch typically occurring between parents and babies, or between lovers; or faster, a type of touch more common between strangers. We found that slow, caress-like touch was more likely to communicate love, even when the touch was delivered by a stranger. In contrast, participants didn't attribute any special meaning or emotions to touch delivered at fast velocities. Interestingly, in the case of brain damage involving the insula, people have difficulties in perceiving affective touch, as well as disturbances in the sense of body ownership. This suggests the existence of a specialised pathway that arrives from the skin to a specific part of the brain.

We exchange tactile gestures as communicative tokens not only to build social bonds, but to establish power relationships. In professional Western contexts, people typically apply a certain amount of pressure in a handshake when meeting someone for the first time. A handshake stands as a proxy for competence and confidence; we feel the other person touching us, and ask ourselves: "Do I trust them enough to offer them a job?" or "Should I let them babysit my kids?" One study[14] showed how a firm handshake was a key indicator of success in a job interview, perhaps because the handshake is the very first way that we close the physical gap between us and the other. The handshake is also used to seal an agreement, with the force of a signature or contract. The danger and vulnerability that's intrinsic to touch is part of what allows it to serve this socially binding function; indeed, it's believed that the handshake arose as a way of ensuring that the two people involved weren't holding weapons.

The language of touch also affects the way that we relate to ourselves and our bodies across the lifespan, with profound impacts on our psychological wellbeing. In another set of studies, we investigated the way in which people with anorexia nervosa perceive caress-like touch as compared with healthy people. Anorexia nervosa is a severe eating disorder characterised by a distorted sense of one's own body, but it can also lead to a reduction in social interactions. We wanted to understand whether the fact that sufferers report finding less pleasure in social interaction might be related to the disorder. Across two[15] studies,[16] we found that people with anorexia perceived slow touch delivered with a soft brush on their forearm to be less pleasant, compared with healthy participants. Importantly, we found the same pattern of results in people who have recovered from anorexia nervosa. This suggests that this reduced capacity to take pleasure in touch might be more of a stable characteristic rather than a temporary status, related to the severe malnutrition that we observe in anorexia nervosa. This finding, along with other studies, suggests that there is definitely a close link between social touch and mental health. Throughout our lives, we need touch to flourish.

So, what happens to our tactile fluency when we make touch taboo? At the times in our lives that we are most fragile, we need touch more than ever. From everything we know about social touch, it needs to be promoted, not inhibited. We need the nuance to recognise its perils, but avoiding touch entirely would be a disaster. The pandemic has given us a glimpse of what life would look like without touch. The fear of the other, of contamination, of touch has allowed many of us to realise how much we miss those spontaneous hugs, handshakes, and taps on the shoulder. Physical distancing leaves invisible scars on our skin. Tellingly, most people mention "hugging my loved ones" as one of the first things they want to do once the pandemic is over.

Touch is so vital that even the language of digital communication is saturated with touch metaphors. We "keep in touch" and acknowledge that we are "touched by your kind gesture." Some researchers have suggested that technology could enhance our physical connection with others, prompting new kinds of interpersonal tactile connections via hug blankets, kissing screens, and caressing devices. For example, a project based at University College London is exploring[17] how digital practices such as "Likes" and emojis—signals that communicate emotional states and social feedback—could extend to the remote manipulation of textures and materials. Two people at a distance could each have a device that detects and transmits tactile feedback: for example,[18] my sensor could become warm and soft when my partner on the other side of the world is available and wants to let me feel their presence, or, conversely, it could turn cold and rough if my partner needs my presence.

Nothing can compare with the magic of a physically intimate moment with someone.

There's a lot of potential for these devices, especially for touch-deprived people such as the elderly, people who live alone, or children in orphanages. Consider that 15 per cent[19] of people worldwide live alone, often far away from loved ones, and that statistics are suggesting that more and more people die alone, too. What a difference it would make to have the possibility of being physically close, even when far apart.

However, these devices should be complementary to the power of a skin-to-skin tactile exchange, rather than a substitute for it. Nothing can compare with the magic of a physically intimate moment with someone, in which touch is often accompanied by a cascade of other sensory signals such as smell, sound, and body temperature. Touch is physically and temporally proximal, in that it means "we are close to each other, and we are here now, together." Unlike other senses that can be digitalised, such as seeing someone's face and talking to them over Zoom, touch requires you to be in the same place, at the same time, with another human being. A digitalised version of touch would be missing this rich sharing of a specific moment in space and time, allowing a more limited experience of what a hug could provide. If I could potentially pause or retract from someone sending me a digital caress, that aspect of touch in which we "feel along with another person" would fail.

In the current environment, is the idea of a "renaissance of touch" just for the brave and the foolish? I don't believe so, and scientific evidence speaks loud and clear. We lose a lot by depriving ourselves of touch. We deprive ourselves of one of the most sophisticated languages we speak; we lose opportunities to build new relationships; we might even weaken existing ones. Through deteriorating social relationships, we also detach from ourselves. The need for people to be able to touch one another should be a priority in defining the postpandemic "new normal." A better world is often just a hug away. As a scientist, but also as a fellow human, I claim the right to touch, and to dream of a reality where no one will be touchless.

NOTES

1. Tiffany Field, "Touch for Socioemotional and Physical Well-Being: A Review," *Developmental Review* 30, no. 4 (December 2010): 367–83, https://doi.org/10.1016/j.dr.2011.01.001.

2. Monica Anderson and JingJing Jiang, "Teens, Social Media and Technology 2018," *Pew Research Center*, May 31, 2018, https://www.pewresearch.org/internet/2018/05/31/teens-social-media-technology-2018/.

3. Nicolas Guéguen and Céline Jacob, "The Effect of Touch on Tipping: An Evaluation in a French Bar," *International Journal of Hospitality Management* 24, no. 2 (June 2005): 295–99, https://doi.org/10.1016/j.ijhm.2004.06.004.

4. H. T. Chugani, M. E. Behen, O. Muzik, C. Juhász, F. Nagy, and D. C. Chugani, "Local Brain Functional Activity Following Early Deprivation: A Study of Postinstitutionalized Romanian Orphans," *Neuroimage* 14 no. 6 (December 2014): 1290–301, doi:10.1006/nimg.2001.0917.

5. Julianne Holt-Lunstad, Timothy B. Smith, and J. Bradley Layton, "Social Relationships and Mortality Risk: A Meta-analytic Review," *Public Library of Science Med.* 7, no. 7 (July 27, 2010), https://doi.org/10.1371/journal.pmed.1000316.

6. M. Eaton, I. L. Mitchell-Bonair, and E. Friedmann, "The Effect of Touch on Nutritional Intake of Chronic Organic Brain Syndrome Patients," *Journal of Gerontology* 41, no. 5 (September 1986): 611–16, doi: 10.1093/geronj/41.5.611.

7. Kerstin Uvnäs-Moberg, Linda Handlin, and Maria Petersson, "Self-Soothing Behaviors with Particular Reference to Oxytoxin Release Induced by Non-noxious Sensory Stimulation," *Frontiers in Psychology* 5 (January 12, 2015): 1529, https://doi.org/10.3389/fpsyg.2014.01529.

8. Laura Crucianelli, Yannis Paloyelis, Lucia Ricciardi, Paul M. Jenkinson, and Aikaterini Fotopoulou, "Embodied Precision: Intranasal Oxytocin Modulates Multisensory Integration," *Journal of Cognitive Neuroscience* 31, no. 4 (April 31, 2019): 592–606, https://doi.org/10.1162/jocn_a_01366.

9. Alberto Gallace and Charles Spence, "The Science of Interpersonal Touch: An Overview," *Neuroscience & Biobehavioral Reviews* 34, no. 2 (February 2010): 246–59, https://doi.org/10.1016/j.neubiorev.2008.10.004.

10. Francis McGlone, Johan Wessberg, and Håkan Olausson, "Discrimina-

tive and Affective Touch: Sensing and Feeling," *Neuron* 82, no. 4 (May 21, 2014): 737–55, doi:10.1016/j.neuron.2014.05.001.

11. Letizia Della Longa, Teodora Gliga, and Teresa Farroni, "Tune to Touch: Affective Touch Enhances Learning of Face Identity in 4-Month-Old Infants," *Developmental Cognitive Neuroscience* 35 (February 2019): 42–46, doi:10.1016/j.dcn .2017.11.002.

12. Laura Crucianelli, Lisa Wheatley, Maria Laura Filippetti, Paul M. Jenkinson, Elizabeth Kirk, and Aikaterini (Katerina) Fotopoulou, "The Mindedness of Maternal Touch: An Investigation of Maternal Mind-Mindedness and Mother-Infant Touch Interactions," *Developmental Cognitive Neuroscience* 35 (February 2019): 47–56

13. Louise P. Kirsch, Charlotte Krahé, Nadia Blom, Laura Crucianelli, Valentina Moro, Paul M. Jenkinson, and Aikaterini Fotopoulou, "Reading the Mind in the Touch: Neurophysiological Specificity in the Communication of Emotions by Touch," *Neuropsychologia* 116, part A (July 31, 1018): 136–49, https://doi .org/10.1016/j.dcn.2018.01.010.

14. Greg L. Stewart, Susan L. Dustin, Murray R. Barrick, and Todd C. Darnold, "Exploring the Handshake in Employment Interviews," *Journal of Applied Psychology* 93, no. 5 (September 2008): 1139–46, doi: 10.1037/0021-9010.93.5.1139.

15. Laura Crucianelli, Valentina Cardi, Janet Treasure, Paul M. Jenkinson, and Aikaterini Fotopoulou, "The Perception of Affective Touch in Anorexia Nervosa," *Psychiatry Research* 239 (May 30, 2016): 72–78, doi: 10.1016/j.psychres .2016.01.078.

16. Laura Crucianelli, Benedetta Demartini, Diana Goeta, Vernoica Nisticò, Alkistis Saramandi, Sara Bertelli, Patrizia Todisco, Orsola Gambini, and Aikaterini Fotopoulou, "The Anticipation and Perception of Affective Touch in Women with and Recovered from Anorexia Nervosa," *Neuroscience* 464 (June 1, 2021): 143–55, https://doi.org/10.1016/j.neuroscience.2020.09.013.

17. Carey Jewitt, Sara Price, Kerstin Leder Mackley, Nikoleta Yiannoutsou, and Douglas Atkinson, *Interdisciplinary Insights for Digital Touch Communication* (Switzerland: Springer Cham, 2019), https://doi.org/10.1007/978-3-030-24564-1.

18. Carey Jewitt, Kerstin Leder Mackley, and Sara Price, "Digital Touch for Remote Personal Communication: An Emergent Sociotechnical Imaginary," *New Media & Society* 23, no. 1 (2021): 99–120, doi:10.1177/1461444819894304.

19. Aad Weening, "Households—Global Trends and Forecasts with Respect to Size, Composition and Structure," last modified April 2016, https://iorma .com/household-estimates-2016/.

touch is healing

The Touch Inside of Touch

ROCCO LO BOSCO

After my daughter graduated from college, I left the corporate sector to undertake a second career as a medical massage therapist. Already a certified yoga instructor, personal trainer, and martial arts teacher, I now charted my course into deeper waters, applying a multilevel approach to health and fitness.

During my training as a muscle therapist, instructors mentioned the "mind-body connection," but no one ever spoke in detail about working with that connection through the medium of touch. At that stage of my new career, I didn't think much about the connection myself, since I was encouraged to view the body as an organic machine. From the traditional Western perspective, I learned that soft tissue massage produced a specific mechanical effect that increased blood flow, enabled lymphatic drainage, released spasm, and attenuated inflammation and pain. In other words, touch and "positive thinking" are good for a human being from a psychological viewpoint but incidental to the physical and mechanical techniques we use to treat acute and chronic soft tissue injury and trauma.

Early in my career, which now spans over twenty years, I began working with a forty-seven-year-old female patient—let's call her K—who presented with tendinitis in the shoulder and elbows of both arms. Tendinitis is an inflammatory condition of the tendinous attachments, those end points of muscle where thick, fibrous cords connect muscle to bone. Tendinitis causes pain and tenderness outside the joint. The onset of K's condition had been gradual and persistent, until it became constant, painful, and debilitating. K's pain spiked upon the slightest movement of either arm. She had no prior bodily injury, repetitive motion syndrome, nor physical trauma that might be causatively linked to this condition. In fact, people sometimes develop tendinitis without prior injury. This case, however, proved particularly intractable.

Before K came to me, I had experienced a lot of success in resolving tendinitis in other patients by utilizing certain massage techniques in affected areas. I used everything I knew to help K, with almost zero effect. Up until that point, even in my most stubborn cases, the patient obtained at least a couple days of relief before the pain returned. What normally happens as treatment progresses is that the time interval of relief increases between sessions until the patient becomes pain-free between treatments. The pain gradually abates, and the condition resolves. But even after more than a dozen treatments, K barely experienced even a few hours of relief.

We were getting nowhere. Both doctors and physical therapy had failed to help her. Now my art seemed impotent as well. She was a quiet patient, saying very little during treatment. Taking my lead from her, I said little as well. During the fourteenth treatment, I finally admitted aloud that I didn't think I could help her. She nodded, saying she had been thinking the same thing.

I sat back on the stool and rolled away from the table, looking closely at her. Like so many people, she looked sad. She looked back at me and smiled weakly. Then an odd question occurred to me—one I had never asked a patient before. Had anything emotionally traumatic happened in her life before the onset of her tendinitis? K looked at me wide-eyed, and her right hand went to her chest, covering the area over her heart. She began to sob, an awful, heart-wrenching sound.

"What?" I said. "What happened? I'm sorry. I didn't mean—"

"I lost my son to a drunk driver on his eighteenth birthday last year!" she wailed, holding her arms out before her as she lay on the table. "Oh my God, my arms have felt so empty!"

I immediately began to cry with her. I couldn't help it. We talked for nearly an hour, and I convinced her to see a grief counselor. Seeing a good psychologist after a trauma is a no-brainer, but, amazingly, many people fail to do so for any number of reasons. Luckily, K ended up forming a strong relationship with an excellent psychotherapist, and upon undertaking grief therapy, her condition immediately began to improve and resolved within several weeks. During this time, I continued to work on her.

She became quite a talker, and, of course, she talked mostly about her son and the changes taking place in her life.

Over the years, I have lost count of the number of times I have seen that some persistent and painful physical condition is directly and dramatically linked to a psychological one—even when MRIs, CAT scans, and medical test results indicate an objective basis for the condition. I have also been amazed to see how deeply patients' beliefs about their conditions are related to how they experience them, primarily in relationship to the level of pain, and secondarily to its possibility of resolution. Here are a few examples:

- The man with chronic stomachaches and spasms who finally told me that, while he was growing up, his father had repeatedly told him in disgust, "You make me sick to my stomach!"
- The woman with chronic neck pain with no underlying etiology, according to X-rays, MRIs, and CAT scans, but who had been the victim of a sexual assault while being strangled.
- The woman who developed terrible hip pain and a limp after her best friend, with whom she walked every morning for years, suddenly and without warning moved to another state.
- The man who, after developing a series of diverse and seemingly unrelated physical symptoms that ranged from fulminating acid reflux to lumps in his testicles, consulted with over a half dozen specialists and developed paralyzing anxiety before finally agreeing to psychological counseling for a full-blown existential midlife crisis.

At this point in my life, when I hear the term mind-body connection, I chuckle. There is no mere "connection" between the mind and the body. *Both are two dimensions of a single human entity*, a conscious relational being who is embedded in the world and, more specifically, living in an ever-changing situation. The human mind *emerges* from the human brain and loops back into the body, and the *brain is as much body as any organ, structure, or component*. Though utterly dependent on the concrete corporality of the body, the mind is of a different order than the body—the imaginative and analytical order in which human life, culture, and history occur—and the mind loops back into the body, affecting it in ways that we do not yet clearly understand.

But this loop exists and can be utilized to lessen pain and promote healing. How do we know this? Well, to begin with, we screen every single drug released to market for the "placebo effect" using double-blind studies because *the belief I might be taking a pill that can help me is probably already helping me.* Western medicine *screens out* for this effect. Treating the body as a machine and the mind as separate from the machine, we make little or no use of this effect for the benefit of the patient. Yet variations of the placebo effect can be seen in a variety of medical phenomena. In considering conditions such as hysterical blindness, phantom pregnancy, stigmata, and voodoo death, we can begin to get a sense of the profound interrelatedness of the body and its emergent mind. Other illnesses are related to or worsened by stress, including heart disease, diabetes, asthma, obesity, Alzheimer's, and a variety of gastrointestinal disorders.

What is done to the body affects the mind. What is done to the mind affects the body. The two are no more separate than the thumb and forefinger of the same hand, or the function of two eyes in the perception of depth. What the mind feels as a self and deeply believes will continually and dynamically affect the function and health of the body. The body is not and never was a machine. A machine is made of separate, assembled parts, and its purpose is fashioned by an external agent—the designer and user. A being grows from a whole and carries its purpose within. Beings are wholes that grow into parts. Machines are parts assembled into wholes. Beings reproduce themselves. Machines do not.

The body-mind described here puts the sense of touch in a new and interesting light. We already know through the pioneering research of Harry Harlow, John Bowlby, and René Spitz that physical touch is essential to the physical and mental growth of infants. Without adequate physical contact, infants die. This fact reveals touch as the most important sense, and it is no surprise that, according to studies, the massaging of babies speeds up physical and cognitive development.

I believe that, more than the other four senses, physical touch exists at the intersection of body and mind. Touch locates us on multiple levels. If you touch to care for me, I feel myself right here at the end of your fingers, my thoughts and feelings touched as well. It is the same for you. As I touch patients with my hands, I try to also touch them by deeply listening to them, being alert for subtext or clues involving their physical condition and psychological state. Through touch I collaborate with them in returning to wellness, responding empathetically to their concerns, encouraging their progress, and gently discouraging negativity.

Thus, I have located a *touch within touch*—a way of reaching beyond the skin to benefit what goes on inside it—a touch that is available to anyone who wants to become more intelligent in the area of caring for another. This touch involves forming a relationship in which physical touch is accompanied by authentic and sustained concern for the well-being and growth of the other person, with the understanding that this position is grounded in equality and a sense of humility and openness. Should any benefit result, it will ensue for both parties. It is from this position that physical touch, along with eye contact, facial expressions, gestures, dialogue, subtext, and space between self and other proceed. From this position the being of one moves with the being of another. Touch from without is accompanied by touch from within—the touch inside of touch.

Although I cannot explain "the mechanism" by which the condition of K or other patients has improved, I know that K's son was ripped from her arms, and her arms became sick, that O's best friend suddenly left her walking alone, and so she developed a terrible limp. G was brutally assaulted, and the physical pain continued long after the initial horrific trauma. Moreover, I have no doubt of these three things:

- One's psychological situation affects one's physical situation.
- Utilization of a patient's beliefs in the service of healing is a good idea.
- Healing through massage is best done by encountering and "touching" a patient on a psycho-emotional level.

Speaking of Touch . . .

JUDITH SIMON PRAGER

In times when distance or disease makes touch, the most nurturing of all expressions from the moment of birth on, dangerous, or prohibitive, how can words help us to, as AT&T puts it, "reach out and touch someone?" When we can't touch, words may be all we have.

My professional specialty began as verbal communication: What to say to calm, promote healing, relieve pain, and save lives. Having coauthored several books about the protocol we call Verbal First Aid™ (VFA), I train medical personnel and first responders across the United States and around the world in *what to say* during medical emergencies to ease the stress of trauma and set a course for recovery and healing.

It was when I considered that emotions are called *feelings*, because the experience of them is visceral, that I realized we *feel* them in our bodies. And both touch and words can bring on that experience.

How do words touch the body? A growled "Gotcha!" at the wrong time or in the dark could cause a heart attack. At a difficult parting, "Don't leave me, please don't leave me" could cause rivers of tears to flow. A joke that "really tickles" you might cause a fit of uncontrollable laughter so that you can hardly catch your breath.

Compliant victims of stage hypnotists, nervous to have been selected, are made by words to feel the sun forcefully beating down on them. As a result, they start perspiring and removing their clothing. It's the sense of touch the words convey that starts the stripping.

Why? In VFA we explain that people in fear, pain, emergencies, or crises slip into an altered state of consciousness, the organized, rational prefrontal cortex of the brain being hijacked—that's the word that's used—by the primitive, emotional, limbic part of the brain. They may present as unfocused, and in that altered state it is as if they were in a trance, where words can become suggestions to the unconscious mind.

There are myriad ways that the magical words of VFA help people heal. For our purposes here, let's move away from emergency situations to times—too often these days—of anxiety, depression, loneliness, and frustration, the host of emotions that a simple hug might ameliorate or alleviate. And if we can't hug those who are suffering, only see them on a screen as if through a window, no touching, what can we offer?

Imagine or remember a time when you were frightened or abandoned and felt a single gentle pat on your upper arm, perhaps a moment of soft eye contact to go along with it, and heard the words "I'm right here. Let me help you."

Essentially then, words—ah, here we are—can act as suggestions or commands to the available unconscious mind—which is why Verbal First Aid™ is so effective in the midst of a crisis.

So how do we use words, images in the mind, to hug someone who really needs it through the screen? There are several techniques, some psychosensory, such as emotional freedom techniques (tapping) and Havening Touch™, that can bring words, images, metaphors, and touch together.

Mirror neurons are theorized by neuroscientists as cells in our brains that are activated both when we generate a movement and when we watch someone *else* move in that way.

Imagine that, literally.

You know the phenomenon of the contagious yawn that circles the room. Of the irresistible laugh. Most charming of all, we've seen the mother feeding her baby in a highchair, tilting the spoon toward the child, and opening her own mouth. Likewise, we actually flinch upon watching someone fall down a flight of stairs, almost as if we were the one falling. We seem to all be in this together.

In other words, mirror neurons may collapse the distinction between what you *see* and what you *feel*.

The therapeutic practice known as Havening Touch™ applies here because it literally calls up the sensation of a hug. Even the name evokes "safe haven," which is what it allows. It uses words, yes, and touch. If you were with me in my office, I might apply the Havening Touch™ to you. Or, more pertinently here, you might do it to yourself facing me, as I demonstrate it.

You would watch me crossing my arms in front of my body and placing my hands on my opposite shoulders. Try it. Then slide your hands down along your arm to your elbows. Even if you're only imagining it, can you feel the hug-ness? Back up then to the shoulders and down again to the elbow and repeat. The theory is that such movements, like the earliest touch of a parent's arms holding you, may allow healing brain function changes to occur that shift the way you hold trauma and make it possible to find relief and even a new level of comfort.

Rubbing your hands as if you were rolling a little glass marble between your palms, and even stroking your forehead and cheeks also can evoke this response.

It's been my experience that you can mirror comfort with a friend on Zoom or Skype while saying words such as, "You are safe, you are loved, you are protected, you are seen, you are appreciated"—whatever words resonate. Or even having them say, "I am loved, I am safe," if that wording works, which allows them to imagine you touching them.

This simple *self-havening* aspect of Havening Touch™ (*https://havening.org/*) does not remove old traumas, as Havening Touch™ techniques do in therapeutic circumstances, but self-havening can be very self-soothing and can help bring people back to calm.

And the suggestion of my words, even as you read them, may have brought that literal feeling to mind so that you felt them at some level. The sensation of touch is that powerful, that grounded in our experience, that familiar.

Touch, physical touch, is the universal metaphor for gentle care and concern. Yet I began thinking about the *body of metaphors* for subtle human touch, not body or limb manipulation that involves osteopathic or chiropractic techniques or massage, helpful as they are.

This is where the abstractions begin, so that when I express something tender, something caring, you might likely respond, "You have touched me deeply." That response signifies that I expressed a feeling, a sentiment, a calming phrase, and you *felt* it. "Your words; they touched me." "I am so moved by your loving words." Or even "What you just said touched my heart." My heart!

This is where the touch metaphor reaches its wildest dimension. You're likely responding to something I said that had nothing to do with insinuating a physical touch of any kind. You're only acknowledging the positive emotion I communicated, that triggered a positive emotion in you. And you translated the abstract communication into the metaphor of physical touch. "You touched me; your words have touched my heart."

This is the core dynamic of Verbal First Aid™. I can communicate a positive emotion that can have the effect of "touching" you, and the touching can begin the trajectory of healing. It happens within the metaphor. It happens with the impression of touch within the altered state that's triggered in those moments of trauma—when the touch of Verbal First Aid™ is most needed. And the healing begins.

Yes, COVID-19 strictures confine many of us, keep us separate from those we care about and would otherwise hug when we greet. Even when the pandemic subsides to the point where it is safe to venture back into the world, there will still be times when the interaction of physical touch is not available. The power of thoughtful caring words, and the overpowering metaphor of touch, as we've just now explored, exists for everyone.

Touch, a hug, can transform physical sensation into communicated feelings: "You can breathe easy now" or "I love you" or "I'm right here."

Words can do exactly the same thing in reverse: transform communicated emotions into visceral, bodily feelings. "It moved me when you said that."

What we're hungering for is closeness, connectedness. Havening Touch™ (through mirror neurons) and words offer ways to nourish that yearning. *Touching is feeling, and you can emulate that feeling with words.*

Touch the hearts of others. We always have that power, can call upon touching words to connect and confirm we're all in this together and we're all going to figure out a way to get ourselves to safety.

Ink

WILL JENNINGS

"O, Honey . . ."

I was on a gurney and just wheeled into the operating theater, somewhat unclear about who had been cast in the antagonist role until the cheerful anesthesiologist welcomed me in an optimistic major-key-toned preview of what's about to happen next and his part in that process. Halfway down his second or fourth line in the script, he'd used a phrase ending with ". . . then we'll intubate you."

I'm not a doctor, but I have gone through certification as a wilderness first responder, a regimen chockablock with ACRONYMS you memorize to help you memorize, so you will routinize your response to the potential for gore, the urgent and furtive you will be summoned to calm and navigate with confident banter interlaced with questions and answers you will track in elapsed time. I am methodically rooting about for what senses can surmise; probing for landmarks and clocking patterns of a story unfolding into complication more quickly than expected.

You train tone present without prejudice, to palpate and reconnoiter with your fingertips and eyes. And your ears.

Even through the pre-op diazepam haze, I distinctly heard the stage direction through cheerful monologue abruptly end in the word "intubate." This sparked a training-installed synapse to dash through rote-cached acronyms and quickly latch on to memories of checklists where *that* word was not a good place to land.

"Wha . . . wait . . . intubate? Thassnotasuchgood . . ." They'd upped my dosage a notch.

Then I noticed my surgeon, clean, shiny, uncapping a Sharpie, seriously confident, but cracking the slightest of grins. The necessarily present others softly chuckled or nodded.

They were the protagonists. *I* was the one who'd arrived to complicate on cue, to be exposed through their rehearsed motions and internalized script.

The anesthesiologist softly leaned into my face, looking a bit fish-eye-lensed to me by then, and said, "Trust me. You're gonna wanna be asleep for this."

And that's when I felt "O. Honey."

She was enclosing my left hand, warming it so that I hadn't even realized how cold it was in that time and sterile place. Her hands were so soft, even through two layers of nitrile gloves, or maybe it was her eyes looking at me through a plastic shield, some combination of the two. "You are loved, and we will protect you from all harm."

Actually, I may be making up most of that last quote, because this was a Catholic hospital and I'm pretty sure by her knowing exactly when to cup my left hand to warm it, especially with her eyes, she was the sort of nurse who was also the sort of nun whose timing was miracle enough.

What should have been on the routine side of complex quickly turned into the complicated and more urgent realm, where order and routine would be restored through skilled hands and clear eyes. Instead of going home in three to five, I remained in post-op care for a full twelve days, each of them a constancy of hands so knowingly placed.

Two years past, my belly wears a nine-inch vertical scar that neatly half-rounds past my belly button. If anyone asks me if I have a tattoo, I answer, "Yes."

Sometimes they ask me, "Where?"

"A day in late October," I say.

And as often, "Lettering? Or art?"

"Art," I reply.

"Of what?"

"Touch."

The Healing Power of Touch

CHRISTINE PAGE

Are you a natural toucher? I am.

Whether it's a handshake, hug, or gentle touch, this somewhat re-served Brit has always known that touch is essential to my wellbeing, communicating more meaning than words. Many of my happiest memo-ries involve touch, whether being engulfed in love by my hugging aunts, shifting from scared to invincible as my father took my hand in his, or the feeling of freedom as my body swam through warm Mediterranean waters. The last memory of my mother was the knowing touch we ex-changed when she had too little breath to talk.

Probably because of my upbringing, it's felt natural to include touch in my work as a holistic doctor, knowing its power to heal body, mind, and spirit. Whether lightly stroking a patient's shoulder to reduce anx-iety, offering a comforting hug to a grieving relative, gently massaging the hands of an old woman as she speaks of her loneliness, or rubbing the feet of preterm infants, willing them to live, I've always seen touch as the most important of all the five senses and the one we least want to lose.

Indeed, touch is the first sense to develop in the embryo around six to eight weeks of life. Through varying densities of nerve endings in differ-ent areas of the skin, the nervous system is informed of our emotional and physical environment with exquisite precision. With our eyes closed, we can tell, with 75 percent accuracy, whether a simple touch on our arm is being delivered with love, anger, assertiveness, or sadness.

Loving touch is designed to bring us comfort and security through the bonding hormone, oxytocin, which in turn reduces stress and enhances the optimal response of our immune system to deal with infections. Oxytocin is produced whenever we feel close to someone, but the levels we're able to produce and evoke in others are dependent on the bonding we received from our mother in the first few months of life. Having delivered many babies, I'm in awe of the way a mother naturally knows to place her baby close to her heart, gently touching its beautiful body, looking into its eyes and whispering sweet words of comfort. When this is continued on a regular basis in the first year of life, the result is a well-balanced, much loved, secure individual who enjoys social connection. Sadly, when this is absent, there's a tendency toward aggression, lack of trust, and social isolation.

However, even if such early bonding didn't occur, all is not lost. There are plenty of ways we can enhance our oxytocin levels. We develop trust, first of ourselves and then of others. With love, we can start to notice when we're lost in our thoughts and gently re-enter our body. Perhaps we simply start to feel the texture of the ground under our feet, the warmth of the sun on our body, or how the chair we're sitting on has the strength to support us. It's also nurturing to massage one arm with the fingers of the other hand, noticing the tenderness of both giving and receiving.

Then we're ready to take trust to the next level by scheduling regular massages, making sure we voice what parts of the body need attention. I love head and foot massages, as they always seem to quiet my over-active mind. Apart from sharing massages with a partner, young children love giving and receiving massages, a wonderful way of helping them to relax before bed. And what if your closest friend is furry? Stroking our pets enhances our oxytocin levels beautifully, and they in turn have appreciative ways of showing their pleasure.

I've come to see that the recent pandemic is a blessing in some ways, as it's highlighted what we had almost forgotten: the essential elements to ensure our health and happiness. There's no need for us to buy them or for science to develop them; they are our birthright as human beings: touch, smiles, laughter, confidence, compassion, and the knowledge that we bring value to our community.

Over the past decades, I've watched as we've moved further from these essentials, with 'touch starvation' becoming a real psychological condition for people of all ages. For many, technology has become their most intimate friend. In fact, it's sad to say, we probably touch our computers and phones far more regularly than we do our loved ones.

Maybe this is the time to take the opportunity to restore common sense to the way we look at health, focusing less on the germ and more on the soil, our innate knowledge of what feeds and nurtures body, mind, and spirit. A touch, smile, eye contact, heartfelt conversations, and encouragement seem such humble offerings, but they can make a world of difference.

the sanctity of touch

Socks

MEG KEARNEY

My father's body has ceased to shock me.
His skin runs over his bones like a slow
river, rippling where belly meets hip. We've
learned how to hold him: one arm each around
his back, one hand under each thigh; Mom
and I stand on opposite sides of his
bed and, on the count of three, lift him
onto the bedpan. We close our eyes—
Dad, then me. Oh, he pants, it's so damn cold
as I tell myself, *I am not the first*
daughter to do this. Afterward, Mom pulls
his gown down over the stones of his hips
while I train my eyes on the Gold Toe socks
I'll later steal, when Mom gives away his suits.

Famine

BEATRIZ TERRAZAS

In the last months of her life, when she could no longer speak, my mother began reaching out to touch the faces of her loved ones. The first time she gently lifted a hand to touch my eyelids, it was startling. I was sitting next to her; she patted the tips of her fingers over my nose, then my cheeks and my lips, the way a person with no sight might understand another person's features. I don't know why she felt compelled to do this. Alzheimer's had taken her voice but not her sight. Maybe it had to do with the disease stealing her memories. She could no longer ask, "Who are you? Are you my daughter?"—so maybe she had to get to know each face all over again in the only way she could.

When she finally lay dying at home, with her brothers, sisters, nieces, and nephews stepping in to say goodbye, my father, long divorced from her and having since reared another set of children, squeezed next to me in the narrow hall outside her bedroom. There was a sense of urgency as he whispered, "*Se puede pasar a tomarle la mano?*"

Years of cached anger boiled over and sloshed into my grief. After all this time, he wanted to hold her hand? To touch her? Why? They must have been happily married at one time, but I couldn't remember him ever touching her face. I carried no memory of him smoothing her hair behind her ear or taking her arm as they crossed a street. Still, in hindsight, I realize that he, too, had been her family, and I'm ashamed of the chill with which I answered: "Ask the nurse, she's right there."

He stood by the bed and held my mother's hand. Between his palm, warm and calloused from years of work, and her palm, cool and mottled, a faint purple from her slowing heart, there must have passed a thousand unsaid words. Messages spoken by skin on skin. *Remember when we met? That dance where you thought I was asking your friend to dance? It was you. Remember when I said those awful words to you? I'm sorry. Forgive me.*

I survived sexual assault. I don't touch easily. Nor do I allow it easily. Sometimes the intimacy of touch—that skin on skin—overwhelms me.

But during the dementia journey, I held my mother's hand when we walked the neighborhood. I wiped her chin after she ate, made sure there was no toothpaste on her face after she brushed. I helped her clean up after she went to the bathroom, bathed her when she could no longer do it herself. Afterward, she allowed me to dry her off, running a towel over her back and down to her feet. With a wide-tooth comb I untangled her hair, careful of her scalp, careful not to cause her pain.

That night when she was dying, as her breathing became more and more shallow with each passing hour, my siblings and I held vigil by her bed. We squeezed her hand. We smoothed her hair away from her forehead. We kissed her.

Every so often, I opened her lips to place a drop of morphine on her tongue.

Until she no longer needed it anymore.

Years later, in the wake of a global health crisis, I obsess about touch. Obsess about the memories of that night, and the significance of being able to hold the hand of my dying mother, of being able to hug the others who, with me, bore witness to her final moments and shared in my grief.

After she died, the nurse put a stethoscope to her chest and documented the time. Then we stepped out of the room to let him prepare her for the mortuary men who would arrive a bit later.

Were his hands gentle despite the fact that she no longer felt his touch? Despite the late hour—it was almost dawn—did he pause to observe the sacredness of the moment? As he ran a cloth over her eighty-four-year-old body, did he still feel a sense of awe at the geography of skin? Did he note the history in wrinkles and sagging flesh, the secrets contained in scars and a missing nail?

Was he humbled by the privilege of skin on skin, despite the absence of life?

Especially in the absence of life?

———

A late spring day in 2020, my husband and I were out walking. A couple rode past us on a tandem bike, a blue vintage machine that complemented their youth, as did the casual scarves around their necks so that they looked like a magazine cover. They stopped to talk to us across the blacktop, they on their side and us on ours, all of us observing the strict six-feet-apart protocol of the times. They were German, a couple studying here in Texas. He was intrigued by the Leica I carry, so I asked them to smile and took their photo. They described the front deck of the house they were renting and gave us directions so we could visit when it was safe to do so. We parted, and I was filled with a sense of nostalgia.

Back at home, looking at the photo of their smiling faces as they stood by that blue bike across the street, I was suddenly exhausted. Exhausted by the separation between humans in the wake of a pandemic. Sick of attending work meetings, and family meetings, and board meetings on a computer screen. Sick of living in a famine of human contact, with a hunger that fills the spaces between our bodies. I had wanted to cross the street to meet this couple. I had wanted to shake their hands, to let him hold my camera and turn the focus ring, unafraid of the space that we shared.

And as I sat at my table, I pictured all things human and messy, all things life-affirming that I miss in this famine. Things like holding hands. Or like laughing so hard with my sister that I find myself reaching out to touch her on the shoulder. Or like eating with friends, passing the butter and wine, reaching to tear off a piece of bread at the same time, our hands colliding without fear. Because we know that even an inadvertent touch from another person can be a sacrament.

Considering the Defense Production Act

DANIEL B. SUMMERHILL

> The defense production act gives the president several powers
> to ensure that supplies for national defense are produced by
> U.S. industries and distributed to places that need them.
> —*Washington Post*

before bed, i tell my daughter i love her for the 11th time
today & her mouth yields: daddy, you're a builder!

i take inventory of the day, reckoning the bookshelf i built
next to her bed, holding each nail near the head, i consider
my grandfather, his unfailing advice and swing
from the elbow once more, like he taught me—

i haven't felt the effects of the defense production act except
through my grandmother-in-law's hands & all the other
grandmother hands that still have breath. how
they've stopped manufacturing prayers briefly to manufacture

face masks, how in some cultures, mouths don't
mouth i love you. i think how we are made holy
not by our hearts, but through our hands. i press my lips
together, take my fingers to her cheek, as if to say—

Rain Passing

BECKY KENNEDY

Deep June and the evening
doors, the stacking of the dusk.
Birds drop back: the quickening,
the press of leaves, flowering
of the huge unconscious rain,
the heavy peonies, rain-
blackened branches lost in the
forest of the swept glass. You
don't need to see to know what
belongs only to leaving:
silencing of rain's broadcast
across the dark grass and the
coveys flushed and rising, the
cold shine. Wide sound of sudden
endlessness: you don't need to
look to see a thing that's gone:
passing luck or love or the
one you'll never touch again.

Nothing Was Gone

BECKY KENNEDY

Late enough: the darkness at
your feet. The evening doors that
opened to the shade shifting
the edges of the grass. And
moved against the lilac bent
to the window where you watched
the children, their cheeks alive,
asking why is there night and
the window filled with sky and
everything was everything,

which was the night. After he
died, the night, listening for
the waiting river of the
trees. The morning when nothing
was gone, the night-blown poppies,
forsythia opening
its yellow rows. Murmur of
motors like rain, the ardent
rain giving itself until
everything touched everything.

Mami's Touch

MARÍA LUISA ARROYO CRUZADO

BAY STATE MEDICAL CENTER |
AFTER MIDNIGHT, MONDAY, MARCH 7, 2016

I sit with Papi in the Bay State Medical Center ER, holding his right hand, his body bucking with hernia pain and his mind delirious. My touch isn't the one he wants.

For the three weeks leading up to this night, the night he will die, he is hospitalized first at Mercy. A Medicare patient on dialysis, a double amputee legally blind and with a pacemaker, he languishes there for two weeks. Despite my advocacy and frequent visits, specialists don't consider his medical situation severe enough to warrant a transfer to Lahey Clinic in eastern Massachusetts for specialized care. When one specialist observes, "He looks like my father," I retort: "God help your father if this is the way you'd treat him!"

Before her March 2 brain surgery for trigeminal neuralgia, Mami visits Papi every day at Mercy. As she's been doing for the last ten years after she quit the factory work she loved, Mami washes his face and body tenderly. Knows how to coax him to balance on his side to wash his back. Pats his body dry. Massages the front and back of his legs with lotion, including the round stumps below his knees. Mami then sits within holding-hand distance, talks to him to make him feel loved and less alone. Nights, I bring her home.

The last time Mami touches Papi is at Mercy. Before her brain surgery. Before his transfer to Lahey Clinic, where his type of medical insurance doesn't guarantee quality care. Before he's transported back to Springfield to die.

CURRAN JONES FUNERAL HOME |
FRIDAY, MARCH 11, 2016

On the CD the funeral director plays on a loop, Papi's fingers play the *cuatro* as Colón's tenor fills the air with the *boleros* my ears have heard since I was in Mami's womb. Papi's casket, open.

I stand first in the receiving line. To my left, Mami sits exhausted, recovering from brain surgery. As each guest comes forward, I lean in and whisper: *"Por favor no beses a Mami."* Her face is too tender to tilt up for kisses. She offers her hands.

Miranda's wife—I forgot her name, but I remember her love for Bacardi—kisses me on both cheeks. As we hug, I whisper, *"Por favor no beses a Mami. Tuvo cirugía."*

"What if I kiss her, touch her? What'll you do about it?" she smirks in English.

"Do it and I'll kill you." My eyes black stones.

She jumps back from me. Slides to the left to touch my mother's hands, her eyes flitting between me and Mami. Her lips offer forgettable *condolencias*. Moves on to hug my two grieving brothers.

OAK GROVE CEMETERY |
SATURDAY, AUGUST 1, 2020

Before COVID-19, Mami used to walk to Oak Grove Cemetery *"para visitar los que no ven,"* to visit those who can no longer see. Her ebony walking stick with the red handle and her white fluffy hair recognizable as friends driving by would offer her a ride. Shaking her head, she'd respond, *"Quiero andar."* Even before Papi's death, Mami walked regularly to Oak Grove to pray at the headstones of loved ones, their graves divided into neighborhoods marked by Springfield street names.

Since March 2020, the caretakers have closed the Bay Street entrance. The main entrance is too far for Mami, seventy-five, to reach in this summer heat. Sometimes, my brother Mel takes her. Today she asks me. Once I drive through the stone arch, my car meanders toward the Puerto Rican neighborhood of graves.

Masks dangling from our wrists, Mami and I gingerly walk among the headstones to Papi. We are safe with one another. I live upstairs in her two-family home, shop for both of us, and check in on her almost daily.

Whenever I do, I greet her with my hand over heart as I ask for her *bendición*. "*Dios te bendiga*," she responds, hand over heart.

Every time she visits Papi, Mami inspects the headstone she bought for both of them, rinses it with bottled water from the dust or dirt that clings to the red India granite. She rubs Papi's ceramic photo, talks to him with the same soothing tone she used when he was alive. She traces the carving of his *cuatro* with no strings. Lays her hand on top of the grave heated by the summer sun to pray for him.

Touch Haiku

ALICIA OSTRIKER

What is touch? A child
in an airport hugs grandpa's
legs. The grownups smile.

Braiding my daughter's
hair, drawing the strands along
my palms, smelling them,

that's all in the past.
But my husband's whole body
is in the present.

Holding my mother's
hands, singing you are my sun-
shine, her favorite

song, while she died, how
grateful I am, that moment
years back, is present.

What a privilege
to lay hands on those coming
into our world, and

The Sanctity of Touch

those taking their leave
or those who have made children
with us—privilege

unavailable
if it is covid taking
your beloved ones,

when there is nothing left
to smooth over except
your own empty hands

My Father's Room

FAYE RAPOPORT DESPRES

When I pick up a pen that sits on my father's desk I think, *he was the last person who touched this.* It's been six years since he died, but only now, in the middle of a global pandemic, has my mother decided to sell the house. She has been in assisted living for more than a year, and she is finally ready to let go.

My mother never entered my father's room after he died. His room was part office, part former bedroom. A lifelong insomniac, he needed his own space, something he couldn't have dreamed of as a child in the camps during World War II.

After fifty-seven years of marriage, I assume my mother couldn't handle seeing or touching the things he left behind. Once or twice, she asked if I would go through his room with her, but I wasn't prepared to deal with both her emotions and mine. So she never leafed through his files or examined the collection of leather wallets he kept in a drawer. She never picked up the small spiral notebook in which he wrote a few thoughts, his handwriting shaky from the Parkinson's. All of that was left to me.

My father used to wrap me in bear hugs so tight that I couldn't breathe. He wasn't a tall man, but he was thick and muscular. He had gained weight after arriving in America as a refugee at the end of the war. I don't think he ever got over the astonishing availability of food.

I hated being choked by my father's hugs, but any resistance to his effusive demonstrations of affection offended him. When I think of the strength in his arms, I have to force myself to remember his last days. In the nursing home, my father, so powerful in body and mind all his life, could no longer hug anyone, or walk, or feed himself.

I contemplate both versions of my father as I stare at his desk. The calendar on the wall says it's September 2013, the last month he was home and in this room. As I reach for various items—wooden letters that spell "Ben," a carefully sharpened pencil, photographs he'd been sorting and planning to frame—I can't escape the thought that he was the last person who touched them. His DNA is likely still on them. I wonder what he was thinking when he set down the pencil for the last time or placed mail from an insurance company on a plastic letter tray. My father intended to revisit each of these items, but he never did.

I slide the desk drawers open one by one. I pull out files and mementos and arrange them in cardboard boxes on the floor. I notice two silver Stars of David tucked into a plastic bag and wonder what my father would have thought of everything that has happened since he died. Could he have fathomed a neo-Nazi protest and counterprotest in North Carolina or a president who would say there were "very fine people on both sides?"

And despite all he had been through in his eighty-four years, what would my father have thought of COVID-19? No one could have envisioned the stay-at-home orders, the toilet paper disappearing from supermarket shelves, the breweries producing hand sanitizer. I find a pile of matchbooks with logos from his favorite restaurants stored in a wooden cigar box. How sad he would have been to see those restaurants shuttered and dark, no host to greet him with a handshake and a hearty, "Good evening, Dr. Rapoport!"

I swivel back and forth, dwarfed by my father's office chair, again surveying the items on his desk. I reach for a small white box; it has Hebrew letters on it and contains a sugar substitute. He must have brought it home from one of his trips to Israel.

Before I picked up that box, my father was the last person to touch it. I wonder if something left by his fingers is transported onto mine. I wonder if somehow, by picking up his things, I can still touch him in a way. The thought reminds me of the way I run my fingers over photographs to try to touch the arm of a person I once knew, or stroke a beloved pet long gone.

Cardboard boxes filled, I stand and walk to the door, scanning my father's bookshelves as I go. *The Chosen* by Chaim Potok. A weathered collection of Russian literature. Thick tomes about art. A book that details the resistance mounted by Jews in Poland, where my father was born.

The swastika startles me. *Mein Kampf*, by Adolf Hitler.

Why would my father, who was haunted by memories of the camps all his life, have that book? I don't know, and I can't ask him. Shuddering, I move on.

At the door, I turn and look back. My father's desk looks bare, hungry for what it has lost. The boxes sit on the floor. The room is no longer the way he left it.

Nothing is.

What I wouldn't give for one of his bear hugs now.

Bridge Strike on Storrow Drive

QUINTIN COLLINS

Metal touching metal,
gnarl me into wreckage, shear my scalp from
my skull as we collide. My
sides bulge then break. All my
cargo scatters beneath
this bridge so sudden: my produce
crates, bed that
slept in many apartments, now
debris on Storrow Drive. This overpass—
why do I always
bring the fire to your I-beams?
Smoke and oil, lights and
sirens, congestion and car horns.
I don't interrupt
traffic flow just to mar your paint.
I like your graffiti
more than clearance
signs. You hover
over space where rain
stops for a moment; your shadow
could embrace my side view
mirrors. Look,
you are the bridge.
I am the truck,
foot to some floor, still

heaving as a heavy thing does. I
     race to crash. These many Septembers
when my metal met your
                  metal, guts and gears
     swept to the shoulder. Not the
collision or clash; it's my hoping
     each time, if even for seconds, that
          I'll coast under your steel, that
you will be my shelter.

As Long as I Know You

ANNE-MARIE OOMEN

I stand in the foyer in front of glass doors and stare into the long hall at the Oceana County Medical Care Facility. At the far end, an aide rounds the corner and there comes Mom, small as a cloud in the distance but rolling ever closer in her Breezy wheelchair, her blue patterned comforter over her knees, her white blouse stretching across her tummy, distorting the embroidered pastel flowers. The aide pushes her close to the door, and I touch the glass. She does not move but looks at me quietly.

"Hi, Mom. Happy Birthday."

My mother turns ninety-nine today. April 28. Early spring or late winter in Michigan, same difference. A day cold and dreary as a fading spirit in the wind. Mom does not walk, does not talk much—only a few words. She is incontinent, has a suprapubic catheter, is fed by the staff, is blind in one eye, and is unable to answer any but the most scripted questions. We do not know how she continues. We do not know how to live with the fact that she continues.

Long ago, when all the legal stuff for powers of attorney was done, she established one single criterion for living: *As long as I know you* is what she said. And for a long time, longer than it should have, that criteria held like a vine to a wall. But now, *as long as I know you*, once hailed for its clarity, has revealed its vagaries, its blue-toned uncertainties. Because it turns out, a grey zone wafts there, a half knowing on her part coupled with an unknowing on our parts. What if sometimes she does, and sometimes doesn't, and what if it's different people at different times? And what if we do not really know her for who she has become now— does the reversal hold true if she's not the woman who was our mother?

"Knowing" is an uncertainty roiling inside our visits. Knowing is not knowing.

And then the pandemic. Before the pandemic, there were days when she helloed me by name from across the day room, and also days she knew me only if I pulled my chair so close our breaths mixed. I took her hand, said my name, introduced myself again. The touch did it, brought us back together: that flicker of acknowledgment like heat lightning in the distance. Her one good eye would take me in, appraising like a judge again, then that half-smile, recognition—as we sat close, fingers intertwined. We were back at the farmhouse table of childhood, sorting buttons from the button box, matching the pairs, or in the garden, handing off the basket of beans, smiling at abundance.

As she's aged, it's been different for each of my siblings. Now Tom and Rick say she doesn't know who they are at all anymore. Pat is far away in Colorado but says that when she and Duane came to visit Mom last summer, Mom was happy to see her. Called her by name. In that visit, Pat and Duane played fifties dance tunes and danced in front of Mom, and she watched them and laughed and was present. But later, when I asked Mom if she had seen Pat, Mom didn't know. For years now, Marijo and I have made weekly visits to Mom, Marijo more often. Marijo says mom sleeps most of the time they are together—so she doesn't know. These days, Mom knows only me. Sort of. This hurts Marijo, and we have tried to figure out why—or if I am even reading the signs correctly. Because I am the oldest? Or because I take her hand, rub her skin gently, and repeatedly tell her stories about her own fields, about the farm and the gardens, the past that once was hers. I say over and over, often the same stories, "Remember Mom, when . . ." She once looked straight at me and said, "You're the one who remembers things . . ." but she didn't sound happy about it.

Now, Mom's birthday, April 28 in a year like no other, a year that, between pandemic and social unrest, defies the order we thought to live by. I last saw Mom nearly three months ago when, in early February, I visited with her favorite non-cafeteria lunch, McDonald's fries and one of those dried-out cheeseburgers that when I warmed it in the microwave released its smoky scent. I cut up the burger into eighths, squeezed the pieces closed so it became gooey finger food. She picked up the pieces and lifted them, trembling, to her mouth. She made that murmuring sound like a dear animal at feeding.

Mom is at the glass. She stares through tempered windows, looks at me as though she should know me. The aide adjusts the chair so Mom sits sideways, closer, can see better. She looks unsteadily in my direction, through the glass. The glass is clean, reflections play in and out. The words "Automatic Door" form a decorative barrier between us. My hand presses against it as if I could reach through: *as long as I know you.* Will she, after all this time? My fingers smear the surface.

I left her in early February. I flew to Guatemala, an annual trip. When I traveled, which was often, my greatest dread was that she would die or take a turn. I checked with Mom's nurses as often as I had service. *She's fine, the same.* She had been so long in decline that her slope had nearly leveled, and the incremental losses were almost immeasurable, and this passed for stability. *Go,* they said.

None of us counted on a *novel flu*, that first innocuous moniker.

We—I was traveling with my husband—heard the rumors while we were in Guatemala City as a blip on our radar. Yes, concerning, but gosh it was flu season, wasn't it? We were careful, washed our hands, used sanitizer. But as days passed and we listened to international news, the tone shifted like an acrid wind. Reporters, journalists, regular folks were speaking of rising cases, a much-more-serious-than-the-flu virus in China, Europe, and then the United States.

They were overreacting. Weren't they?

But as David and I watched the numbers grow, watched the disaster of testing and not testing and unreliable testing, of overwhelmed ERs, and people dying, we realized—not an overreaction. I heard for the first time the phrase "flattening the curve." Was it then I grasped that the world was about to change?

Despite cost, I called the medical care facility every day. *How are you* all *doing?*

Yes, she's the same.

No, no one has it. Yet.

One morning, the radio blared that the World Health Organization had declared the virus a global pandemic. I lingered over the word "pandemic," strangely new and biblical at the same time—pandemics were about plagues. We don't have plagues in this world. Do we?

Then the president declared a national state of emergency. Then we knew for sure. We had to get back to the United States. During the flurry of packing, I realized that once home, I'd still have to self-isolate—because we'd been in Guatemala, so two more weeks before I could see her. Keep her, them, us, safe. Hard but doable.

As I stuffed the suitcases, Marijo's number showed up on my cell. Marijo rarely called when I was on the road.

Hello, hello, what's wrong?

Mom's fine, but the gist: Mom's facility would quarantine—not just a couple of weeks but a full-scale lockdown, visitors forbidden, which now looked to be months, not weeks. I could not see, not touch my mother at all.

And now, her birthday. April 28. Almost three months. Marijo and I phoned each other that morning because Mom no longer used the phone. We both teared up. I asked if we could meet, go to her bedroom window and sing, take a balloon. Marijo said maybe, but I could tell by her voice that it would be harder for her to see Mom behind glass than not to see her at all. Let alone touch her. After I hung up, I sat on the couch and sipped cold coffee and let the silence ripple. David looked up from his computer news and said, "Yeah, you should go anyway."

Which is how I ended up driving two hours to the facility on highways nearly barren of traffic, stopping only once at a garden nursery with partial staff, and, masked up, pointed to a tiny blue globe vase planted with moss. With gloved hands, they lifted and wrapped and carried it to the curb, where I picked it up. Through long miles, I thought of her days like moss in a blue globe.

What was this that was happening to her, to all of us?

When I pulled into the parking lot of the facility, I wrapped the vase in disinfectant wipes, put on my mask, and called the nurses. I was buzzed into the enclosed foyer, the glass laden with signs warning of the automatic door, now latched, of the quarantine, the lockdown, that residents could be reached via FaceTime. Protocol and procedure.

She's at the glass.

"Hi, Mom. Happy Birthday," I say again.

She can't hear well through glass. She looks at the aide and the aide repeats, "She says happy birthday, Ruth."

My mother looks back at me, says, "Oh. Thank you." Proper.

I'm alone in the foyer, and there's cool outdoor air, and so I take my mask off, hoping that will make the difference.

She studies my face, studies the glass, studies my face again. She is trying to figure it out—who I am.

"It's Anne-Marie," I say, "It's me." A ridiculous thing to say.

She says nothing. Am I blurred, distorted like one of those carnival mirrors?

I launch an explanation, where we've been. Then simplify. We've been away. The aide repeats everything slowly because not only can't Mom hear, but she looks as though she does not understand.

I say, "I'm sorry we couldn't come sooner. Because of this sickness."

When the aide repeats, Mom turns her face away, doesn't speak. She has that look: she's supposed to say something but she's decided to keep her mouth shut on purpose. She's like that in times of uncertainty.

I tell her about the plant, the blue globe and the delicate moss. I show her through the glass. I tell the aide I'll leave it wrapped in the wipes on the table, and when I go, she can pick it up, use the extra wipes I have not touched, and give it to Mom. She promises.

I tell Mom about the garden David and I have begun, and I remember aloud her own garden, the spring plantings, the raccoons that took all of our sweet corn just as it ripened the year I was ten. She glances sideways at the aide as if to ask *who is this nut?* I tell Mom about David—thinking she may remember, connect, but she doesn't respond. Her lids go heavy.

I ask, "Mom, how old are you today?"

When the aide repeats, Mom opens her eyes. She thinks. She says, "About eighty."

I tell her she is ninety-nine today.

She speaks suddenly, vehemently, "Oh no." She looks at me accusingly, then down at the comforter. She plays with the hem of the blanket, running anxious fingers on the satin. If I could just touch her, could hold her hand again after all these months, could breathe with her, would it come back as it has before? Would she be at ease, say my name?

Suddenly I'm sure the pandemic, the quarantine and lockdown, has done what plain time could not. We are severed; we cannot touch, and thus she has forgotten. In the larger scheme of national death and illness and loss, what happens between my mother and me is the smallest thing. An ordinary thing, this forgetting. But it feels large, as I see too how that long-ago criteria *as long as I know you* holds her and us in thrall, a new immensity. If the virus or anything from plain flu to kidney failure strikes, we let her go. We let her go in this time when we cannot touch her. Could I do that?

The aide is bored.

Unable to go further, I tell the aide I will say goodbye now. I raise my voice, project, *I love you, Mama.* The aide repeats it all, *she loves you.* An echo without inflection. Mom does not respond, even when the aide repeats *Mama*—this from a daughter in her sixties. I thank the aide and turn to leave, then turn back and try to sear her face in my mind, the pale skin, the crown of white hair, the weary blue eyes. I wave. No response, but just as I turn to press the exit button, her voice rises clearly as water in a stream, as clearly as if she *were* merely eighty, "Thanks for coming, honey."

I stand, stilled and stunned. The aide smiles.

Honey is not my name, but no one else in the world calls me that. No one could—I wouldn't let them. No one else could say that line and make it be a golden thread. Because whoever I am to her, it means this: she may not see Anne-Marie, the daughter she named for a biblical mother and daughter, but she sees me as an intimate, and uses the endearment reserved only for those in the family. My name may be gone, but the sweetness of the tribe, her inner circle, remain in that term, "Honey." In this time when bonds between people starve for connection, when they thin to barest threads, this is invisible touch, a mere two-syllable touch, the touch that leaves one hungry for more. At the same time, it is enough—it has to be. And this paradox, this impossibility of touching, but doing so with a single, clichéd endearment, is how we know each other now. I leave the plant but carry this away—her blessing to me on her ninety-ninth birthday, her touching gift.

Touching Lois Goodbye

LINDA DEFRUSCIO-ROBINSON

At the top of the list of the many things my sister and I had in common was the fact that we both worked in beauty. Lois was a master barber/hair-stylist, and I am a licensed electrologist, aesthetician, and master barber, along with certifications as a dental assistant and laser hair removal technician.

Lois owned her own salon for thirty years. She had an associate who did men's cuts and a few other stylists for women's, and a huge clientele. Whenever I went to visit her and found her running behind, I grabbed a hair-cutting cape and a pair of scissors and went to work at her side.

Lois was good company, and it was always festive in her shop. Some of her regulars had been coming for so long that they knew not only all the staff but many of the other clients. Her shop was a meeting place, a hub where you could get a good cut and catch up on the neighborhood buzz at the same time. No matter how you came in, you left smiling.

Lois first noticed tremors in her hands in 2011. Though she was diagnosed with Parkinson's disease, she didn't imagine for a minute that she would have to give up her work anytime in the foreseeable future. She was young, only fifty-four at that time. Except for the Parkinson's she was perfectly healthy—and always on the move. When she wasn't on her feet cutting hair, she biked, swam, or walked on the beach with friends. She prepared food and helped out at her local homeless shelter. She loved to serve people. By fine-tuning her meds, her healthcare team made it possible for her to continue to go about the business of living her life. If anything, her shop became even more spirited after her diagnosis, because in addition to her staff and clients, friends frequently dropped by, just to check on her. Even her healthcare providers popped in now and then to say hello.

Then one day while she was styling one of her regulars, Lois began to feel faint and had to lie down to keep from passing out. Her blood pressure had dropped.

Her diagnosis was reevaluated, and her doctors concluded that what she had was not only Parkinson's but also its crueler cousin: multiple system atrophy. MSA is rare. Statistics vary, but most agree that about one in fifteen thousand people get MSA compared to the one in six hundred who get Parkinson's. MSA is a degenerative neurological disorder affecting automatic functions such as blood pressure, bladder, muscle control, and breathing. Treatments are available, but there is no cure. Those who get it have a shorter lifespan than most Parkinson's patients.

I remember the day we got her diagnosis. "How long?" she wanted to know. "If you make it five years, it will be a miracle," the neurologist told her. She turned to look at me. We stared at each other for a long time. She didn't cry. Lois had never been a crier, even as a little kid. Eventually she dropped her head.

Lois's balance became an issue, but she did not close her shop. She simply let her staff do more of the cutting while she scheduled appointments and helped clients make decisions about style and color options. When I went to visit her, I brought fresh flowers, half-moon cookies from the bakery, mac and cheese—or some other concoction I had cooked myself with her in mind: comfort food. I also gave her manicures, pedicures, foot massages, and minifacials.

Lois was two and a half years younger than me, and we had been giving each other beauty treatments all our lives. We had learned these skills initially from our mother, who had been an electrologist and who cut and styled hair for family and friends. It's no wonder that we both wound up in the beauty industry. You could argue that being concerned with beauty makes for a superficial career, but our mother would tell you otherwise; she would say that it is never superficial to make people feel better about themselves. You can have all the degrees in the world, but if you don't get to touch your clients, to tilt their chins or run a brush through their hair, you're missing out on something special. When you do the kind of work that my mother did—that Lois did, that I do—you are touching people all day long. In this world where the number one method of communication is texting, a gentle touch can win a heart. Lois loved my massages and nailcare rituals, and I loved administering them.

When Lois could no longer walk or drive, the shop was finally sold, and I began to go to her house to see her. Her medical team had arranged for 24/7 care, but the caretakers were rotated, and only from time to time would I see the same person sitting beside her when I visited. In total, Lois had over fifty caretakers from several different service agencies. She also had a close friend, Scottie. Ten years before he'd been a customer in her salon, then he became her handyman. When she got sick, he became an almost constant companion and caretaker.

As Lois declined, her doctors arranged for a massage therapist to come twice a week to help with muscle stiffening and circulation issues. When she could no longer speak, her speech therapist provided her with a whiteboard with the alphabet and numbers on it. By pointing to one letter at a time, the caretakers and I could figure out what she wanted to communicate. S.O.C.K., for instance, told us her feet were cold and she wanted someone to put her socks on. Or, if she had them on, she was warm and wanted her socks removed. With all the time and energy devoted to communicating her most essential needs, there wasn't much room left for her to tell us what it felt like to be inside a body that was barely functional. She was never a complainer anyway.

Greg, my husband, and I made a slide presentation for her. It began with her father (we had different fathers) and our mother on their wedding day. Then came Lois, the baby. Lois at her birthday parties, Lois at graduations, Lois modeling, Lois skydiving, Lois at work, Lois at home. She always did up her house and yard on holidays. Her favorite was Halloween, when she got out the hay bales and the scarecrows. When there was no holiday, she brightened the place up with flowers. The flowers were often gifts from friends who knew how much she loved them, but when friends didn't buy them, she bought her own. She wanted to marry before she died, and Scottie wanted that too. At the end of the presentation there were pictures of Lois on her bed in her beautiful wedding dress, on her wedding day.

Lois, who never cried, cried the day we showed her the slide show. Her shoulders didn't jerk; her mouth didn't turn down; her expression didn't change at all. It couldn't. Her muscles could no longer support any such gestures. We only knew she was crying because the tears kept on coming.

I asked her if she liked the presentation. She blinked, many times over. Multiple blinks meant yes, very much.

In the last year of her life Lois went on a feeding tube. By then she couldn't move at all, not even to point to a letter on her board. The only form of communication left to her was the blinking. It was like visiting someone in a coma—except worse, because while Lois's body was all but paralyzed, she herself remained conscious of her suffering. It took me about thirty minutes to get from my house to hers, and I prayed the whole time, both ways. On the way there I prayed for a miracle for Lois but also for more practical things: a good visit, that I would say and do the right things to help her relax, that the caretaker on duty would be someone I liked spending time with. On the way home I prayed for peace and grace.

One day I arrived and found Lois in tears again. I asked the caretaker if she had any idea what was wrong. She didn't. Lois's medical bed was in the living room. I put the flowers I'd brought in a vase and placed the vase on a shelf where she could see it and sat. "Are you happy to see me?" I asked. She blinked. That told me my presence had nothing to do with her tears. "I love you," I said. She blinked again; she loved me too. "I love you more," I continued. She blinked again, but still she continued to cry.

I looked her over. She was well-groomed as always, wearing clean clothes. The caretakers gave her a shower twice a week, using a medical hoist to move her in and out of the stall. She was thin but not terribly thin. "Are you in pain?" I asked. She blinked again. "Okay, let's figure out what's wrong," I said.

I began at her feet. "Do your toes hurt? Your ankles?" Nothing. Her feet were okay. "Your calves, your knees?" I checked her urine bag. It was clean. I checked her catheter. Everything looked good. "Is it your stomach? Your heart? Your arms? Your shoulders?" Nothing.

Finally, we got to her head. "Do you have a headache?" Nothing, she didn't have a headache. "Mouth hurt?" No, mouth was good. "Teeth?" "Eyes?" "Ears?"

And there it was! She began blinking madly. "Your ears? Something is wrong with your ears? Is it an itch?" She blinked and blinked and blinked.

I found myself in tears. Lois had communicated her problem to me, and I was in a position to solve it. It might seem like a trivial happenstance, but it felt monumental at the time. I left the room and returned with Q-tips. She blinked when she saw them. Gently, I cleaned both ears.

Then I wiped her nose with a tissue. I hugged her. Later, while I worked on her fingernails and toenails, I told her stories, one scary one—because Lois loved a good horror story—and one with a happy ending to balance things out.

It would be another six months before Lois died at the end of 2017, six years after her initial diagnosis. But it was on that day, the day Lois's ear itched, that I came to believe Lois and I had experienced some measure of the peace and grace I'd prayed for.

touch is not
always human

Spice

DAMIAN MCNICHOLL

There are some who claim dogs can't express love, that they're incapable, and that the face licks and smiles we're convinced we see when they greet us are artifice, a survival trait they've learned while lying beside humans at campfires over the eons in an effort to gain our favor. Those folks insist that canines are pack animals who demonstrated essential subordination to higher-ranked members of the pack in their wild past by copious licking, averting of the eyes, and exposing their vulnerable bellies to prove they weren't a threat, and that domesticated dogs exhibit similar behaviors to those humans whom they consider to be above them in the family hierarchy.

Ever since my boyhood spent in the purple-heathered hills of war-torn Northern Ireland, I've mulled the question of whether dogs are capable of loving humans in the same way we love them. Certainly, the position of pets has changed in society, and we routinely accept now that our dogs are important family members. Only the fusty law regards them as chattel still so that, when animal abusers are prosecuted and found guilty, they're merely fined and not given the long jail sentences they truly deserve. The question first burned in my mind when I got my first dog at the age of five, an adolescent Jack terrier with one erect ear and one floppy one and whose name I can't remember because he didn't live with me very long. Unfortunately, he was mischievous and loved to chew holes in socks and shoes until my exasperated mother, not a dog lover, gave him away to someone when I was at school. He was my first love. I huffed, wept for days, and informed Mother that I'd never forgive her and was running away from home.

The question reignited on the arrival of my next puppy, after much ne-
gotiation and vetting by Mother, when I turned seven. It was love at first
sight. I loved Sheila infinitely more than I loved my four siblings, espe-
cially my annoying youngest brother, whom I reprimanded frequently
every time he attempted to claim her tail-wagging affection. Unfortu-
nately, like my chomping terrier, the border collie's stay in my life ended
abruptly when she slipped her leash one afternoon in my uncle's com-
pany, ran into a field pocked with nervous sheep, and unwittingly proved
herself to be an excellent shepherd dog by rounding them into a perfect
circle in ten seconds. It didn't matter that Sheila was talented enough to
take part in televised sheep trials after she'd been properly trained or that
she'd sell for a tidy sum, and I could have a small share of the proceeds.
Uncle William's very suggestions seemed wicked. What was money in
comparison to love? I retreated to my bedroom determined to remain and
die there, refusing to eat for two days until Mother baked a raspberry and
cream sponge cake I loved.

My last boyhood dog was a corgi-terrier mix, and I chose blindly to be-
lieve Sandy loved me to the commensurate degree I adored him. I will-
fully purged from my mind his traitorous running up to Mother and re-
maining loyally by her side every time she appeared in the backyard. In
fact, Sandy was the poster doggie for the theory that dogs can't love hu-
mans, that their shows of affection are indeed artifice. Mother fed him
but showed him scant affection; rather strict she was and did not allow
him to sleep in our house (his place was a kennel in our garage). And yet
he regarded her as the alpha. Years later, another dog buttressing the the-
ory was Maxx. When my youngest sister and her family adopted an intel-
ligent border collie mix from a local pet shelter, he treated their ten-year-
old son Ryan as beneath him in the family ranking. Maxx refused to obey
Ryan's commands yet eagerly did what Ryan's older brother asked him to
do; he would not leave a chair he was lying on and knew was Ryan's when
the boy came into the room to sit; and he only allowed Ryan to pet or play
with him when he was in the mood, snarling or baring his teeth to warn
him when he'd had enough. The situation resolved only when my sister
and her husband showed him regularly that he was the lowest-ranking
member, taking him to an outside kennel where he never liked to stay to
cool off every time he bossed or acted aggressively with Ryan.

My question about whether dogs can love was finally answered when
Spice entered my life, albeit the answer came six years after first meet-

ing him. I fell in love with his master, and Spice, a seventeen-inch-tall, brilliant white Cockerpoo with champagne-colored ears and a stubby tail that feathered beautifully, came as part of the package. I'd emigrated to the United States in the early nineties and met Larry two weeks after my arrival. Invited to spend a weekend at Larry's Bucks County home, Spice dashed around a corner and bounded across the kitchen floor toward Larry, braking so sharply on the Mexican tiled floor when he saw me that he slid and crashed into my leg.

Being half poodle, Spice had hair—not fur—and the softest curls I'd ever touched. Not even the girls I'd dated when trying futilely to persuade myself that I was heterosexual had hair as soft as his. As I petted him, a sweet perfume imbued with an acrid undertow of veterinarian clinic wafted up from the shampoo Larry used to bathe him, and the warmth of the dog's body raced up my fingers directly into my heart. His amber eyes were soulful and wise. I thought him beautiful.

I hadn't owned a dog since Sandy had died. Fifteen years earlier, he'd been monstrously killed at the hands of patrolling British soldiers who poisoned dogs with baited meat to stop them barking while the soldiers eavesdropped at the homes of families in the nationalist area where I lived. By my fifth visit to Larry's home, I was as deeply in love with Spice as I was with his owner. I also began to notice Spice was different from other dogs I'd known: he looked me straight in the eye as if he were human, displaying neither aggression, submission, nor discomfort as our peering turned into stares; and he didn't touch. I'd hold out my hand and he'd sniff, his mottled pink nose wrinkling comically at its tip, but he made no attempt to touch it. Of course, he exhibited the usual canine proclivities, liking to be petted on his back and chest, having his ears scratched and leaping skillfully into the car when he figured we were going out for a drive.

"I don't think Spice likes me that much," I said, as Larry and I lay on the bed watching television late one afternoon.

Spice had just shaken off my hand, leaped over Larry's belly, and stretched out beside him in that manner so common among cocker spaniels, his back legs splayed out as if he were about to start swimming the breaststroke. I thought this very cute. He glanced over at me as if wanting to judge my reaction to his treacherous act, then turned away and lay his chin on top of his front paws. I was miffed at the ungratefulness. Larry tolerated having his dog—although I was secretly thinking "our" dog by now—on the bed, only because he knew I liked to have him beside me. We were still in the honeymoon phase of our relationship, that time where each partner's dislikes are suppressed, and all wishes are granted.

"Why do you say that?" Larry asked.

"He never licks me." I sighed. "He knows me three months now. Not once has he tried to lick my face or hand. Even when I feed him."

Larry guffawed.

"What's so funny?"

"Haven't you noticed he doesn't jump up on you, either?"

Larry sat up on the bed and stroked Spice's lower back, causing one of the dog's back legs to jiggle uncontrollably. "He used to lick and jump on everyone when he was a puppy. A lot of people don't like that. Especially older ones. I hate dogs doing it. So I trained him not to put his paws on people's chests or lick."

"I've never heard of a dog not licking."

"It wasn't easy to make him stop."

I laughed. "Well, don't try training me not to do stuff I like if we ever live together."

He chuckled, then asked if I wanted to move in.

Long after the honeymoon ended and for years thereafter, I'd try to tempt Spice to lick my face on the sly. He'd hold his nose so close to my cheek I could feel his hot breath. But just as I anticipated his wet tongue, he'd turn away or regard me in puzzlement. I couldn't believe such discipline. It wasn't that he never disregarded other parts of his puppy training. Often, when we returned from visiting Larry's mother in New York City, we'd discover the garbage pail in the kitchen overturned, gnawed pork bones strewn over the floor, butter wrappers licked clean, and a sheepish Spice peering guiltily out from behind one end of the kitchen island. He'd bound across the lawn on spotting a deer, ignoring Larry's commands to return, his head and bent forelegs making him appear like a gazelle as he leaped across the tall grass. On occasion, he broke Larry's cardinal rule, disappearing with Louis, the oldest dog in the neighborhood, for hours after Louis came calling in the yard looking to corrupt Spice. He knew breaking this rule would result in physical punishment, yet he broke it more than once. But never would he lick or touch my face. Not even dabs of maple syrup or ice cream worked.

Over the years, Spice's allegiance changed from Larry to me. It miffed

Larry when we first noticed, although not unduly, since he loved us both. The reason I became master was the oldest in the world: I now fed Spice. I'd stopped working as an attorney in the city to stay at home and write a novel, so it made sense that I took over the domestic chores, and this included feeding the dog. If I went upstairs, Spice went upstairs. If I went to the basement, Spice went to the basement. If I was taking a jacuzzi, Spice lay at the foot of the bath. If Larry and I were arguing, Spice disappeared, only to reemerge at my side when I stormed away filled with righteous conviction. Dog experts would undoubtedly say the shift was natural. I was now the alpha in Spice's mind.

On the morning I learned dogs can love humans deeply, I was hurrying from our bedroom on the second floor to the kitchen downstairs. I'd thought I heard someone knocking on the door. Larry had designed and built a custom mahogany staircase adorned with gorgeous balusters that had been removed from an old, demolished mansion in Puerto Rico. Wearing dress socks but no shoes, I slipped on the edge of the uppermost tread, twisted sideways, and tumbled twenty feet to the bottom. Only the feel of the ice-cold marble tiles in the foyer pressing against my cheek stopped me from blacking out.

Spice froze as he regarded me for a long moment and then darted down a short corridor at one end of the foyer and turned left into the kitchen. He started barking. I lay on the floor, my body wracked with white-hot pain. My right elbow felt funny-bone numb. I'd never experienced such pain, not even when I'd cracked a fibula when I was eleven years old. Larry had gone out. The phone, perched on top of a small table that was half-concealed by the large leaves of a dwarf banana plant, seemed impossibly distant even though it was just fifteen feet away.

I heard Spice's nails tapping on the floor tiles as he returned from the kitchen. He circled my body twice, panting heavily, his pupils wide and dark. He drew his face close to mine. I could see confusion or panic in his eyes. He ran back to the kitchen and started barking more furiously. I heard his nails scratch as he pawed the glass pane of the back door. A surge of pain from my side overtook me. I heard myself moan and cry out. Spice raced back into the foyer. He stopped dead at my face and peered at me again, his shoulders bent slightly with helplessness. Another sharp pain emanated from my right side, and I shrieked. Again, Spice ran in a circle around me. I started weeping.

Then I felt something hot and wet against my forehead. I opened my eyes to see a blurry image of Spice's face. It had been his tongue. He'd licked me.

I wiped my eyes. His distraught gaze remained fixed on mine, as if he was trying to judge the effect of the lick. His snout loomed again. I felt his tongue pass over my cheek. He licked not once, not twice, but four times. I was so stunned, I forgot my pain. He pulled his face away and regarded me.

"I'm okay, Boy," I said, my voice a croak.

The lingering feel of Spice's unexpected licks helped diminish the pain in my side as I pressed my palms hard into the cold tiles and dragged myself across the floor to the phone. Relieved beyond belief to grab the receiver, I dialed a friend. Within ten minutes, our friend Lee was there, and she helped me up to my feet.

At the emergency room I was diagnosed with two cracked ribs, given pain medication, and informed that only rest would heal the hairline fractures.

"One way to get out of doing stuff around the house," Larry said, after Lee dropped me at home.

"Don't make me laugh," I said, clutching my side and grimacing.

Spice greeted my homecoming with his usual sniffing and tail wags. It was as if the accident had never happened. He never licked me again. His show of love was a one-off, but it was enough. The question from my boyhood had been answered. Spice lived to be eighteen years old, and when his health finally failed to the point where each breath became a chore, I was able to repay those licks of love. I carried him out to the car and held him during his last car ride. At the vet's office, Larry stroked Spice's side and I talked softly to him as the shot was administered. His beautiful eyes fluttered shut, and he was carried away from his white-hot pain.

Speaking Equus

LYNDA MILLER

I find myself reflecting during this time of COVID on the role touch plays in how we communicate with our human and nonhuman friends. I grew up in the company of horses, and, over more than seven decades, have developed deep and long-lasting friendships with many of them (and a donkey, but that's another story). Learning to be friends with horses has allowed me to witness how they communicate with each other and with humans using touch and other nonverbal cues. In fact, horses utilize a language of sorts, which I think of as Equus.

One of my earliest experiences of speaking Equus turned out to be a vivid example of how *not* to speak it. When I say "speak," I don't necessarily mean with the voice, though vocalizations are part of Equus. Like human languages, Equus employs both vocabulary and grammar, but they're different from what we usually think of when we talk about meaning, whether it's at the word or sentence level or meaning in the larger context of conversation or story. Equus requires the acquisition of what are sometimes subtle and, to humans at least, often obscure aspects of physicality and emotional expression.

When I was about four or five, I was riding Blackie alongside a creek with my dad and some of his friends. I began making Blackie cross back and forth through the water. After four or five crossings, the horse decided he'd had enough. He vaulted out of the creek and streaked back to the barn. I managed to stay on, but by the time we got to the gate to the barnyard I was sobbing and humiliated. What my dad said at the time served as my introduction to Equus: "You can either fight your horse all the time and try to get him to do what you want, or you can learn to think like a horse. Talk like he does. Learn to speak his language."

Thus began my lifelong course in learning Equus, its basic structures and conventions, its nuances and quirks, the meaning of seemingly miniscule changes in vocabulary (e.g., a flickering ear) or grammar (e.g., a series of movements in a particular sequence).

Just as we learn to communicate with other humans through specific linguistic conventions, we also learn to communicate with horses (and other mammals) using their particular communicative codes, touch being of prime importance. Touch—tactile sensation—is one of the foundational aspects of any communication system among mammals, horses included. As prey and herd animals, horses rely on touch to convey information: the location of food, dangers such as floods and storms, the proximity of predators. For horses, touch is a way to connect with their fellow herd members, establish dominance, guide and reassure their foals, indicate safety, and regulate behavior.

As I developed fluency in Equus, I learned how touch, in conjunction with visual, verbal, and attitudinal cues, serves not only as a way to establish a relationship but also as a channel into profound affection and affinity between human and horse.

When I first met NJ, a glistening sorrel quarter horse gelding, he was barely two years old. He was already big, almost sixteen hands (a hand is approximately four inches) and twelve hundred pounds. He was perfectly built for riding in the Colorado mountains where I lived, and for showing in reining horse competitions—events where horses display their athleticism and quiet disposition. Before I made a decision about whether to buy NJ, I wanted to ride him to be sure we were going to be a good fit. His owner said he'd been ridden only once, which meant I needed to pay close attention to NJ's understanding and use of Equus.

When I walked into the corral, NJ and two buddies were watching from the far end. I carried a halter and its lead rope. Rather than walk toward the three horses, I moved away from the gate and over to one side and leaned back against the wooden rails. I rustled together some alfalfa pellets (horse candy) and began humming quietly. After a few minutes all three horses, noses stretched forward, began walking toward me. I put one pellet into the palm of my hand and held it toward the first horse, who came closer, sniffed, then delicately lifted the pellet from my hand. He stepped away, chewing, while the second horse moved closer. I held out a pellet for her, which she took.

Finally, NJ ventured closer, a step at a time, and reached for the pellet. As he lipped it into his mouth, I rubbed my fingers above his nostril, murmuring what a good horse he was. While he chewed, I worked my hand up the side of his head and then behind his ear along his neck, caressing the large muscle supporting the heavy skull. With my other hand, I began scratching his forehead, gently at first, then harder as he leaned into it, while I slipped the halter over his nose and ears. I continued stroking his neck and whispering into his ear, lifting the saddle blanket and holding it for him to smell. Watching his ears, eyes, posture, and tail movements, I saw that he was alert but relaxed. His ears followed my voice and movements while his eyes kept track of what my hands were doing.

Once he'd finished smelling the blanket, I slowly moved it along his neck toward his back. I gently slid it up, so the front covered his withers (the big bone where the neck meets the spine) and the sides were equidistant from his spine. Again, his ears and eyes followed what I was doing. Lifting the saddle resting on the ground next to us, I raised it to his nostril. When his breathing slowed and became shallower, I carefully lowered the saddle onto his back. Then, because he'd tensed a bit while the stirrups settled, I reached forward to stroke his neck and tell him he was doing great. He took a deep breath and sighed, relaxed his muscles, and dropped his head level with his back.

Keeping one hand on his shoulder, I reached under his belly for the cinch and brought it toward me, just barely grazing his stomach with it. His shoulder muscles didn't change tension, so I threaded the latigo (the leather strap used to tighten the cinch) through the D ring on the cinch, tightening it just enough that the saddle wouldn't shift while I led him around in a circle. Once we'd made our circle, I stopped him and pulled a hackamore over his head (a rope halter with only a headstall, headband, and noseband with reins).

By this time, I felt confident we were communicating clearly, all from touching him, not only with my hands but with my arms, my upper body, my face, my voice, and feeling and watching his responses. Telling him what I was doing and running one hand along his neck and shoulder, I used the other to slowly tighten the cinch. Then I slipped my left foot into the stirrup and swung onto his back, first telling him what I was doing.

I sat for a minute or two with the reins loose in one hand, my other hand rubbing his neck in front of the saddle. And then I shifted my weight slightly forward and ever so gently squeezed my lower legs to barely touch his sides, indicating he should move forward, and we walked out into a large grassy pasture.

As NJ walked, I continued rubbing his neck and talking to him. After about fifty yards, I shifted my weight downward and slightly back, at the same time barely tightening the reins, signaling for him to stop, which he did. I immediately loosened the reins and sat up straight, body relaxed and legs resting loosely along his sides. We followed this same pattern for ten minutes or so, and then, as we were walking, I verbally asked him if he was ready to speed up, at the same time shifting my weight forward and to the left, nudging him with my right leg, and he began an easy canter. We made clockwise and counterclockwise circles, stopped, started, became acquainted enough for me to know we were a good match.

In the years that followed, NJ and I explored miles of trails in the Colorado mountains, competed in numerous events in horse shows and rodeos, and became close friends until his unexpected death at the age of twenty-three. He allowed me to explore and utilize the rich and complex features of Equus, including the importance of touch as a basic component of horse-human communication. He also showed me that Equus, like human language, is capable of humor.

NJ had been with me for several months when one day I was rubbing his forehead and he slid his tongue out of his mouth. He just stood there with his tongue hanging out, head lowered, eyes almost closed and ears flopped to the sides. Curious what he was up to, I tentatively reached down and touched his tongue. He jerked it back inside his mouth and grabbed my hand, which he held, gently, for a few seconds before letting go. Then he opened his mouth, yawned, and stuck out his tongue again. This time I put my fingers around it, and again he yanked it back and grabbed my hand with his teeth. When he did it a third time, I knew we had a new game, which became one of many we played for the rest of his life.

While at first I wasn't sure what NJ meant when he slid his tongue out of his mouth, his closing his eyes told me his intention was benign. By dropping his head and flopping his ears, he indicated relaxation and calmness. The combination of those three signals communicated clearly that all was good and that his extending his tongue, while novel and a complete surprise to me, was an invitation to a sequence of play that was unique to our particular relationship.

The human analogue to touching in Equus might be hugging. During this pandemic I've found myself yearning to hug friends, to employ touch as part of my communicative interactions. As I can't use this part of my own language toolbox until the pandemic fades, I am immensely grateful that I can stroke the velvet spots behind my horse friends' ears and around their nostrils, throw my arms around their necks in an embrace, lean into them for support, and feel their strength and power throughout my entire body as we ride along trails beside the river, and I breathe in their unique equine smell and feel their pleasure ripple through their skin as I run a brush along their backs, under their bellies. Judging from what they tell me, we're speaking the same language, and I am a very fortunate human.

touch:
a broader perspective

The Love Compound

RAFAEL FRUMKIN

For twelve years, from the age of eighteen until the age of thirty, I got high regularly. If I got high every day for too many days, I'd stop getting high for a few weeks, like the guys in *Trainspotting*, just to prove I wasn't a drug addict. But unlike the guys in *Trainspotting*, I'd tell myself, I wasn't getting high from "real drugs" like heroin or meth or crack. I smoked weed, crushed and snorted Xanax and Adderall, did party drugs like coke and MDMA and ketamine when the occasion called for them, dropped acid or ate mushrooms when I needed to manufacture an epiphany. These things were all "drugs," sure, but they weren't problematic drugs. One of my friends with whom I regularly got high, a cupid-faced, board-shorts-wearing bro, would say things like, "I don't believe in *self-medicating* or whatever. I believe in doing drugs because they're great." I tended to agree with him. Drugs, as long as they were nonproblematic, were pretty great. This friend and I could do lines until dawn and split a bottle of Jack between us and have great realizations about what wonderful people we were and how much we loved each other and how far the future extended before us, realizations that buoyed me when the only thing extending before me was a toilet's plumbing.

In the summer of 2019, I was using a lot of Adderall and my grandma was barely alive in a hospital in suburban Chicago. She'd had a series of strokes that kept her from talking and seemed to keep her from thinking as well. She couldn't wear her dentures, which meant she couldn't chew, and she couldn't control her tongue or the muscles in her throat, which meant she couldn't swallow. A feeding tube was installed in her stomach. It was impossible to tell whether she recognized us, whether she was smiling or not. She became more a set of autonomic responses than a human being. For several weeks I rehearsed her death. It would happen, I hoped, before the school year began and I had to drive downstate to teach. I would wake up and see my mom sitting on the patio through the window of my childhood bedroom. She would be on the phone, maybe talking to a doctor. I would descend the stairs and wander outside, and my mother would hang up and say "Grandma passed," and I would say "I'm sorry," and she would say nothing, and I would say "I think it's better this way. She was hardly alive, wasn't she?"

But my grandma didn't die that summer. She was transferred back to her nursing home, where she inched along for months, on and off oxygen, beyond speech and facial recognition. When I was a child, she had gone to work for the first time in her life as a real estate agent. She loved the job—she had been an admirer of living spaces long before she'd gotten her license—and I watched as she weaned herself from financial dependence on my grandpa, whose itinerant professional life led to my mother's family being uprooted every few years for job prospects in Michigan, Illinois, Louisiana. From a very young age, I was married to the idea of becoming a writer, and my grandma, who got a rush from showing a house, seemed to understand what it meant to pursue a passion.

"She gets more done before nine in the morning than I get done in the whole day," she marveled when I woke up at six to get to work on my "novel," which was a messy binder full of college-ruled pages about a war between dogs and cats. When I was old enough to understand adult life as more than a set of tedious responsibilities, I began to wonder why my grandma wasn't frustrated that she'd been denied a career. She had retired from her brief stint in realty and was focused, as grandmas tend to be, on the lives of her children's children.

"If you could start over completely and be anything you wanted to be, what would you be?" I asked her. She asked me what I meant, and I explained that, in this scenario, she didn't have to be the one who stayed home with the kids and cooked the meals. She could be the breadwinner out in the world. "Oh," she said, and sat back, smiling. "You know what I'd want to be? I'd want to be someone who loved more. I think there are things about life and people in my life I just didn't love enough. I'd want to be full of the most love I could be at all times." I nodded dourly and didn't ask her to elaborate. I had expected her to say "architect" or "artist" or "mathematician" or something.

Shortly after my grandma moved back to her nursing home, my doctor told me to get sober. He said the drugs were very clearly taking a toll on my mental and physical health. He said this after I came clean when he asked why I looked so pale and purple-eyed and seemed to have lost my short-term memory. This was the first time a medical professional had ever asked me to get sober, and I felt chastened. Didn't he know I didn't do any problematic drugs?

It was *Trainspotting* all over again. I racked up two weeks and then got high. I racked up twenty days and then got high. I racked up fifteen days and then took a trip with the board-shorts friend and did lines in our hotel room in Ho Chi Minh City. I realized that if I was going to make any progress, I'd need to join Narcotics Anonymous. But not even being in the room with other addicts helped: I got a few days under my belt and then relapsed, a few more days and then relapsed again. I narrowly avoided DUIs and possession arrests. It dawned on me that I might actually be a drug addict.

I was still using regularly when coronavirus hit the United States. When my university stopped in-person instruction, I drove upstate to stay with my parents in a last-ditch attempt at getting sober. Not even that worked: I found ways to smuggle Xanax and weed into the house and binge on both. I took thirteen capsules of gabapentin at a time. I had grown so accustomed to how it felt to hold a pill, to pulverize it and snort it up my nose, to feel a drug's pyrotechnic effects on my brain's neuroreceptors, that I didn't know how to live otherwise.

My grandma's nursing home was placed on lockdown. My mom persuaded the nurses to wheel my grandma up to one of the windows so she and my father could stand out front and wave to her. I was too high to accompany them when they did this, and then the nurses wouldn't let them do it again. We had to speak with my grandma via FaceTime, a process that would have bewildered her even if she had been in full possession of all her faculties. We watched her lying on her side, her tongue lolling, her eyes unfocused, breathing heavily, a nurse folding sheets in the background. It was difficult for me. After one such FaceTime, I ran upstairs to vomit.

One morning I woke up and saw my mom sitting on the patio through the window of my childhood bedroom. She was staring at the patio table's surface. I got out of bed and, without changing out of my pajamas, walked downstairs and through the sliding screen door. "Grandma passed," she said as I stepped outside. There had been COVID in my grandma's nursing home. Like thousands of elderly around the country, my grandma was trapped in an environment where social distancing was impossible, saddled with an immune system ill-equipped to fight off a devastating virus. She had passed away while I was sleeping.

"OK," I said, acting how I'd always anticipated I would act. "She didn't have very long left though, did she? She was kind of—she was kind of getting closer."

My mom shook her head, assuming the expression she often did when I'd misunderstood her. "But COVID," she said. "Why'd she have to die of COVID?"

Drugs toy with different neurotransmitters in different combinations. Cocaine is dopaminergic, and alcohol serotonergic. MDMA releases norepinephrine, Xanax GABA. Overwhelming, intense flashes of happiness and then a cratering out, a wasteland of ill-feeling, a need to do more. The bad secret of adulthood is that your neurochemistry will be wrecked by age, and that the hours of euphoria you experienced as a child must now be manufactured for you in brief, synthetic amounts by drugs. Maybe this is a bad secret only drug addicts are privy to.

When I was a child, I stayed overnight at my grandparents' house once a month. This meant I spent a solid forty-eight hours baking cookies and playing hide-and-seek and making mac and cheese with my grandma while my grandpa watched *Seinfeld* in the next room. After dinner, my grandma and I would walk to the park in her neighborhood with a jungle gym that was an incredible metal-and-plastic fortress unlike any I got to play on regularly. I'd climb through the fortress several times before declaring it conquered and then join my grandma on the swings. She pushed me just high enough so I'd get a thrill from jumping off but not so high that I'd hurt myself doing so. The moment when I launched myself from the swing was breathtaking in its lightness and freedom—there was nothing to compare to the feeling of falling forward knowing I'd land like a cat, agile and uninjured, my grandma applauding my acrobatics behind me. I never found the cocktail of drugs capable of recreating that feeling.

Days after my grandma's funeral, I flushed everything I'd been hiding in my childhood bedroom and finally got clean. I thought as I did this of the last time I'd touched my grandmother, how loose and brittle the skin of her arms, how cottony her hair, how flushed her cheeks.

It occurred to me that I hadn't touched her for months—hadn't touched her since Christmas 2019, when we stood around her bed waiting expectantly for her to smile, standing awkwardly aside when the nurse arrived to take her blood sugar. The last people to touch her had been nurses. The last sensations against her skin had probably been latex medical gloves and the aching tug of her feeding tube. I lay in bed thinking about these things, feeling synthetic well-being drain from my brain, wondering if she would forgive me for having behaved how I'd behaved. The saddest thing, I think, was that I knew she would.

Touch means something entirely different to the addicted than to the nonaddicted. Touch is the thing that happens not when you hug someone or trace your finger up their arm or whisper a secret in their ear. Touch is the thing that happens when your drug of choice hits the right receptor in your brain and you feel *capable* of hugging, tracing, and whispering. Touch is done not with fingertips but with chemical compounds. The tactile thrills of snorting, smoking, or injecting are preludes to touch itself. But now, with over one hundred days clean, I understand touch differently. I understand it as the thing that means love between two people. I understand it as freedom, as the moment I landed on the ground after jumping off the swing and turned around to see my grandma smiling at me. I understand it as my grandma posing with her arms around her sorority sisters, or with my mom on her lap, or next to me beside a Lego palace I'd just built. I understand it as a reaffirmation of one's being alive. I understand it as generational, as organically serotonergic, as glue-thick. I understand it as something you barely think about having until you've lost it.

The Imprint of Oral Culture

LYNN C. MILLER

When I was a freshman in college, I found out there was a field of study called oral interpretation, which centered on performing literature out loud. I loved reading fiction and poetry and had been involved in theater by then for years, so I took my first course. That class led to a double major in English and oral interpretation, and later, a PhD in what by then had become performance studies. As I learned how to bring fiction and poetry from the page into acoustic space where works could be heard—and, when staged, seen—by a community of listeners, I became immersed in the ways oral culture and written culture intersect.

In preliterate times, the singer of tales preserved the stories of communities and conveyed them to eager listeners all over the known world. Some of those listeners memorized the tales and repeated them, transmitting the great stories from one generation to the next. Ways of life and their rhythms, heroic deeds, historic figures, and values encoded into stories were passed on. Before print or any other kind of technological communication, the singers, their tales, and their audiences were some of the first systems of how humans kept in touch. The human voice echoed through the early ages of civilization. Before Homer's great epics, when tribes of people were few and far-flung, the magical power of the singers' tales touched societies with the great myths and legends—templates for living.

These stories (*The Iliad* and *The Odyssey* and *Beowulf,* for example) survived and were later recorded in handwritten folios, painstakingly copied in monasteries onto parchment or vellum (often made of goatskin that lasted a very long time), and deposited in the few libraries in the known world. As the monks in their carrels meticulously copied these texts, they sang or spoke the words out loud, establishing the wondrous connection between orality and written culture. The act of writing, whether we maneuver a quill or a pen (later a typewriter, and now a keyboard), integrates thought with the physical body, and is itself a communication, an act of touch. The human voice is encoded both in the body and on the page.

I think of this connection of text and body/voice now during the COVID-19 pandemic, when we are starved for the physical touch of our friends. Instead, we eagerly reach out through emails, phone calls, platforms such as Zoom and FaceTime, and, yes, actual letters and cards. The printing press revolutionized the civilized world in the fifteenth century, making the dissemination of knowledge cheaper and far more accessible, as books were able to be mass produced, reaching large numbers of people.

The book continues to be a most efficient and portable medium. During this time of sheltering, reading is available and surging as a pastime—it's something we can do alone; it surrounds us with a detailed and engrossing new world—one that feels palpable and immediate. It puts us in touch with other cultures and immerses us in other voices, worlds, and psyches. Words on the page are thoughts made material. Words bring thoughts alive: they "sing" on the page and into the reader's ear. We interact with the book in many physical ways, from fingering the paper to turning the pages to flipping back to reread a particular passage. Historian Jill Lepore, in a *New York Times* interview, describes this well when she speaks of a copy of *Little Women* that her mother gave her when she was around six: she didn't like the story, she said, "but I love the physical book, the cover, the smell, the welt on the spine, and that it was my mother's." As we touch the pages in the act of reading, we are in a way sewn into them, our senses awakened by the world we have entered.

Reading, writing, talking, and listening are all bound together. Some of the earliest recorded histories of women were letters, autobiographies, and diaries. Often denied a public forum, women spoke through these private communications: examples include the diaries of a noblewoman in Elizabethan times, Lady Anne Clifford; the diaries of the frontier midwife Martha Ballard in the late eighteenth and early nineteenth centuries; and the slave narratives of the African American Harriet Jacobs in the nineteenth century. Many of these writings were passed on or discovered in attics and cellars, buried in trunks or boxes. These utterances were acts of reaching out, of proclaiming, "I am here, I offer my life in the hope that it will matter." These words, whether spoken aloud or inscribed, are ways of touching. The interaction of writer, text, and reader transforms all three.

Growing up as I did in a very small town in the upper Midwest, the library offered a way into the larger world. Through reading I participated in significant American lives—I remember reading twenty biographies of Abraham Lincoln one summer, mesmerized by his transformation from living in a one-room log cabin, with one year of formal education, to becoming one of the most significant presidents and humanists in American history. When I began to read avidly in the 1960s, I knew few female public figures, but I could read about many in history, activists like Elizabeth Cady Stanton, poets like Gwendolyn Brooks, novelists like Willa Cather. These women, through their words and their actions, spoke to me—as did my teachers, and I had the good fortune to have many good ones. They touched me and shaped my learning and sense of self not by physical communication but by their words and their care in guiding others to find meaning and purpose in their lives. As I taught in higher education for thirty-one years, their voices sounded in my ears and mind. The word "mentor" originates from the character by the same name in *The Odyssey*, indicating a wise counselor, an intimate friend. Mentorship itself is a guiding hand.

When we perform literature out loud and then adapt it for the stage, we expand texts into visual space and into interaction with audiences. Originating solely from the voice in my ear, the scope of performance allowed the text to exist in other physical and aural dimensions. Movement, gesture, and the emphasis of lighting and sound design enhanced the immersion of the perceiver into the experiential world encoded in what had been mere marks on the page. Performance in this way amplifies the reader's experience so that a group of people can immerse themselves in this sensory world as a community. Live performances of every art form grant their audiences the gift of *presence*; each event is special and unique, as it unspools in front of a specific group of perceivers. "Were you there when . . ." someone will ask another about such a live experience. When the person addressed says "yes," an immediate bond from sharing that presence is formed.

In 2000 my spouse and I attended the premiere of *The Laramie Project*, Moisés Kaufman and the Tectonic Theater Project's drama about the aftermath of the 1998 murder of Matthew Shepard, a young gay man. The play was devised through editing and juxtaposing the collected oral histories from hundreds of interviews of people living in Laramie, Wyoming. In the audience with us that night were a number of the people who had offered their testimonies to Kaufman's company. The project combines oral histories distilled into a text, and then a full staging of the stories that immerse us into multilayered perspectives on the tragedy of Shepard's death. The performance, and accompanying talkback, moved us and many in the audience deeply.

The award-winning performer Anna Deavere Smith, an early practitioner of this form of interviewing communities, documented incidents such as the riot in Crown Heights, Brooklyn, in 1991 in her performance of *Fires in the Mirror* and the 1992 L.A. riots in *Twilight: Los Angeles*. Smith, with a rare talent for embodying others, performs each of the multiple and diverse characters herself in her productions.

Many poets and appreciators of the genre believe that poetry can't be separated from the human voice. As in preliterate times, poetry spoken aloud captures the dynamic interaction of movement, sound, rhythm, and meaning. Open mics and poetry slams remain popular throughout the country; some performances incorporate dance and music. Ntozake Shange galvanized the theatrical world in 1976 with her choreopoem *for colored girls who have considered suicide / when the rainbow is enuf*, a production of actors in bright colors (their characters are named after the colors, Lady in Red, Lady in Yellow, etc.) who bring this series of monologues told in poetry to life. As Vinson Cunningham writes in *The New Yorker* of the revival by the Public Theatre in 2019, "Singing and dancing and rigorous listening make up the whole intensely varied texture of the show."

In the late 1960s performance artists such as Laurie Anderson began to immerse audiences in stories enhanced by media, technology, music, and other sound engineering. *O Superman* and *Home of the Brave* are just two of Anderson's productions. Once pioneering, such forms of storytelling are commonplace in the twenty-first century. Even when aided by other art forms, the key ingredients of the creator/deviser/writer, the "text" in whatever form it exists, and the audience remain a constant formula for transmitting stories to keep us in touch with one another. In perhaps a nod to the "happenings" in the 1960s, experiments proliferate with audiences of one and multiple performances where audience members choose which storyline to follow in a kind of hypertext in performance. I suspect that in our virtual world experiments with sensory environments will flourish.

Narrative and story continue to be at the center of culture and of our ways of making meaning, and understanding the world and our place in it. The human voice resonates throughout time, through speech and coded in texts. Old technologies such as the book coexist with newer ones. The eye, the voice, the body are involved in the acts of reading, performing, and understanding. Oral cultures and written cultures intertwine, but both require a relationship between the writer/singer of tales and the reader/listener/viewer. As the author Rebecca Solnit writes in *The Far Away Nearby*, "A book is a heart that only beats in the chest of another." We are continually touched by the wonder of story.

Fingertips Part 3 (with Thanks to Stevie Wonder)

SARAH MCELWAIN

The yoga-for-the-blind class I teach isn't that different from any gentle chair class for people unable to safely get down on a mat. We do breathing practices, rub our energy centers, and move our spines in six different directions. Interestingly, even the most bored teenager asks, "How do you do that?" when I tell them I teach yoga to the blind.

"It's easy. I teach using the fingertips. Most of my students are Braille readers."

The fingertips contain a highly sensitive network of nerve endings that make it possible to detect tiny bumps on paper. Many of my students learned as children to read by touch using this tactile code. Now it's often considered difficult and outdated, replaced by computer audio.

Using the fingertips as a reference seems to work for everyone. I demonstrate: "Your fingertips are pointing to the ceiling (or sky) . . . your fingertips are pointing to the opposite wall (also called extending your Zombie or Frankenstein arms) . . . your fingertips are resting on your shoulders (Angel Wings) . . . or on the outside of your right knee."

If they look interested, I continue: "Yoga is ideal for the blind. Have you ever closed your eyes and followed good instructions?"

Obviously, you don't model. You don't demonstrate or use your own body as an example. You can't show, but you can tell. You can give clear, concise instructions using their own bodies as a reference.

Jimmy, wearing dark glasses, shaking side-to-side like Stevie Wonder, likes to joke that our class is so easy you can do it with your eyes closed.

Getting the class seated is difficult. Our room is not ideal. We meet in a midtown office building with florescent lights and orange plastic scoop chairs. On one side is an intermittently raucous music therapy class, on the other a health and hygiene group. Blind people roam into the room during the class not knowing where they're going.

"Are you here for yoga?" I ask.

Emma gets angry at these interruptions: "Don't they know where they're supposed to go?" she grumbles.

But we practice kindness—*ahimsa*—in the class. Not just to others but to ourselves.

"Wrong room," I say, nicely. They say, "Sorry" and tap back out the door and down the hall with their canes.

At first, I arranged the chairs in a circle. It seemed friendly. But soon I realized the students depended on the wall as a touch-point, using it for stability and a sure sense of place. Now the class sits lined against the wall. I seat them a chair apart to leave a place for their stuff. The blind are generally more worried about their stuff than sighted people. It's a day program and they carry sweaters, sometimes coats, backpacks, fanny packs, bags of food.

"Where's my stuff?" Reaching out to touch their things. "Is my stuff there? Is it okay?" All this stuff must be safely stored and accounted for before we start.

They use canes. Most use one with a tip like a red marshmallow on the end to locate obstacles. These fold in four places and are easily stored under a chair. A few use the long white support stick to clearly identify them as blind or having impaired vision. Red-and-white-striped canes are for the deafblind.

When I first taught this class, I noticed people turning their heads anxiously. "Who's there? Who's in the room?" Not knowing who is in the room doesn't feel safe. It's not ever possible to feel completely safe in a midtown office building in New York City. But there are ways to make a class of blind people feel safer. I say each person's name aloud to let everyone hear who's in class today. After they're seated and their stuff has been stashed, I walk around with a bottle of lavender. Not just for the calming properties. It's a way to say each person's name, ask for permission to touch, and create a sense of safety and control.

In another class I teach, restorative yoga, I never fail to recite, "Keep your eyes closed, this is a hands-on class. I might come around and touch your shoulders or press my thumbs in the lymphatic points along both sides of your spine. But if anyone *doesn't* want to be touched today, it doesn't matter why, please raise your hand. And you can always change your mind later and say *no* when I come around." Only one man has ever raised his hand. Sometimes a few older people in the class thank me. "It's the only time anyone touches me."

In yoga for the blind, I ask every person's permission. "Emma, do you want lavender this morning?" If she just nods, I wait until she says, "Yes." She knows she can say no; she never does. Nobody ever does.

"Is it okay if I touch your hand?" Waiting until she extends a cupped palm, I hold her hand and shake a few drops out of the bottle. This gentle touch is intended to create a reassuring connection and help move the autonomic nervous system from sympathetic, or high-alert mode, into the parasympathetic safety zone. Her hand is soft and childlike, with ragged fingernails and chipped pink polish applied by a high school volunteer.

"Rub the lavender into the center of your palm."

"The sole of your palm," she teases.

This gets a laugh from the class. I once said, "Place the palm of your foot firmly against the floor . . ." while distracted by a person blindly careening through the door with a walker. Sharp-eared Emma riffed on my mistake. Now we have soles in our palms.

Touch is controversial in the yoga world today. I rarely make hands-on corrections. My blind yoga students find them embarrassing. Seating the class apart allows me to sit beside someone and whisper, "May I touch?" Tapping a knee so the hand floating above it knows where to land when we come into the spinal twist. If someone is lost in a free-form arm movement like an Isadora Duncan dancer or waving like a churchgoer while we're doing shoulder rolls, aka Angel Wings, I'm happy to watch their bodies move intuitively in ways that feel good, as long as they seem safe.

A funny story: In ten years I rarely missed class, and I try hard not to be late. It's important to be dependable, someone who always shows up for them. Once when I went on vacation, I told the class I'd bring them back a present, a new essential oil from New Mexico. In the School of Natural Therapeutics store my friend Julie and I blind-tested different blends. "How about this one?" She held another amber bottle under my nose. It was bright but woody and I liked it best of all. It was Kindness. At the counter the clerk asked if I wanted the one-ounce bottle or the larger size. I was flying back to New York. Nobody could remember the TSA limit on how much liquid you were allowed in your carry-on. (The answer is 3.4 ounces or 100 milliliters.) How much Kindness could fly to New York City? We all laughed at this, and I bought the smaller bottle. When I told the class the story, they laughed too.

"Ha! Ha! How much Kindness can you take to New York!" repeated Emma. "Not much!"

"Can't bring too much Kindness into New York City. Law won't allow it," said Jimmy.

I've tried other blends, but pure lavender is least likely to cause allergic reactions. Lavender is an essential touchstone in our class.

"Rub this calming oil into the center of each palm. Use your thumbs to stimulate Lao Gong, the energy center where your healing power is most available."

Next, I say, "Hold your palms near your nose, not touching it but breathing in the lavender. Inhale its healing, calming properties. Let the relaxation process begin."

One of the pleasures of teaching this class, and a reason I stayed for so long, is watching their faces relax. Many blind people don't know or have forgotten how much sighted people monitor our facial expressions. I observe their faces relax in a way that would be rude in a class with vision. Emma's grimace softens. Alice's jaw loosens. Pat sinks. Jimmy sits tall with a broad smile on his face like a contented Buddha. Blinded by a violent attack with a baseball bat at seventeen and a half, he also lost his sense of smell. Scars crisscross his bald head. He assures me that even though he can't smell the lavender, his body is absorbing its healing properties. He is the most highly evolved person I know.

Smell connects to the brain differently than sound, vision, or touch. Known as the primal sense, it activates two brain areas powerfully involved in memory and emotion with both a psychological and physiological impact. If the olfactory nerve and parts of the brain that process smell are damaged, does the signal end? Does lavender have the physiological effect of relaxing the nervous system even if you can't smell it? Jimmy smiles to make me believe it works on some level, even if your sense of smell was beaten out of you with a baseball bat.

We practice *nadhi suddhi pranayama*, or alternate nostril breathing, switching the thumb and ring finger to block off the right then left nostril. Tricky to learn at first, it has become a favorite relaxation technique in the class. Pat asks, "Is it okay to do *nadhi suddhi* when I walk up the hill to church? It calms me down, but I don't want people to look at me like I'm crazy."

"What do you care?" says Emma. "You're blind. You can't see them."

I realize how being so out of touch with the visual world can create a different kind of unselfconsciousness.

We end the class with *namaste*. "The light in me sees the light in you." We press our fingertips together and bow to each other. I like that they can't see me.

It's time for lunch. Jimmy leads, holding the handle of his saintly black Labrador guide dog Houston's leather harness. I line the others behind him, each person touching the shoulder of the person in front. Slowly they file down the hall. Watching them, my hand touches my heart as I get a shot of oxytocin. Not to be confused with oxycontin, it's the love hormone released when you hold a baby against your chest. This sense of well-being lasts all day. There is a reason we use the word "touching" to describe true and deeply felt emotions.

Vast Knots of Miscellaneous Lives

MEG TUITE

Today is pleasurably mute, infused with the stillness of the manswarm. There pervades a comforting lack of voices on a late Sunday afternoon. That point outside when darkness clings to the last strain of light before succumbing to its inevitable aloneness. Bracing itself for that shudder of solitude. Its lonely plight is without fail. The waning hours paint themselves more dismally on this day when streets call out to take refuge in their blank, silent embrace. Maybe a chorus of a million mute cries bank off the muddy puddles, endless rain taps against the panes that stare out with a frightened eye and wonder what it is they must do.

Numberless cold plates sit on tabletops, scattered remains of potatoes, carrots. Endless hands hold forks in bleary kitchens as eyes stare out of icebox windows into other darkened windows. Row after row, street after street, single lit rooms trail one another until each blurs into the next, yet somehow exist apart.

A travesty of foggy dreams splay out into the damp atmosphere, multiply through the soot-ridden avenues. Anyone who dares to walk these sidewalks spirals into cacklings of empty hope. Pedestrians glut with aches of fixations—an invisible collusion links the melancholy plight like holding hands with the ruinous multitude, as though one's own weight wasn't enough.

Rain, winds rise like sounds of Mahler. The winding trances of woodwinds. Battling wail of flutes. Lurk of the brass surrounds.

The sinking doom of another day imprisons us with its rattling monotony, its migraine pace. The conspiratorial rasp of the clock snickers and the numb tread of men loop the same track with impunity.

I sit in my kitchen, fork dangling in my fingers. I look out into the dim light of a kitchen with another hunched figure who leans over his plate, who stares out a window at yet another figure. We watch for the creep of hours like the face of another life. Wonder if we will ever touch again.

Touché—The Internal Touch

DEBORAH SWIFT

In the art of fencing the word "touché" is used to indicate you have been struck by your opponent. It is also used as an acknowledgment of a good or clever point made by one person at another's expense—a kind of verbal slap.

What interests me about the concept in this expression is that it is indicative of both pain and pleasure; the witticism has been received and it hurts, but it's a good pain because it has some irony or quick thinking about it. In sport fencing the term means you have been hit, but everyone knows the wound will never be fatal. In these days of COVID-19 I think it's important to acknowledge the pain and pleasure that we are missing from lack of touch, and that pain and pleasure can be held within the same moment, and held internally, like the expression "touché."

As a writer I am interested in this internal sensation, in the things that "touch" my readers, and most often the touching things in a novel are the ones that contain both tragedy and hope in the same idea. We are moved by the touch of words as if they have transported us literally to another place or point of view. I often use metaphors of touch to describe abstract events so they become more vivid. I find myself writing, "He was struck by how tall she'd grown" or "How was he to handle the call to his mother?"

To feel anything is to acknowledge that we are in debt to our sensation of touch. Every impression was originally a mark made by pressing a hand into some soft yielding material. As a writer, I'm more aware than ever of these resonances of physicality now that they have been removed from us. Yet I'm in a privileged position; I can still touch people, an internal touch with my words, and with my imagination.

Much of our sensation exists in our thought patterns, in what we retrieve from our memories. I remember the touch game we played at a childhood party. It was Halloween and we were invited to reach our hands into a bag to feel what was there. My friend's mother, dressed in a witch's hat made of black-painted cardboard, invited the first child to dip in her hand. Eyes screwed up tight, Chloe reached her fingers into the bag. "The witch's eyeballs," the mother said, with a wicked grin.

The child screamed in gleeful terror and withdrew her hand, hopping up and down in excitement. Of course, we all knew it was a game, but one by one we queued in shivery anticipation to feel these "eyeballs." One tentative touch was enough to cause each of us to scream—except the girl's brother, who drew out one of the cold, wet, slimy shapes to reveal that the "eyeballs" were, in fact, peeled grapes.

The game continued with various innocuous objects, each one designed to provoke more revulsion than the one before. The reason this was such fun was because we trusted there wouldn't be horrible things in the bag, that everything in there would be a pleasant fake, despite what we were told to imagine. And yet when I remember the sensation now, I still recall the realness of the mummy's fingers (twiglets) and the vampire's brains (bread soaked in water).

Touch itself is just touch. We label it after it reaches the peripheral nervous system, which conducts danger signals to the brain. From there, the brain determines whether it will experience the touch as pain. The body can be trained to respond in different ways, to subdue the sensation or enhance it. When I go to the dentist, I breathe slowly to convince myself it doesn't hurt. In the child's game I was able to hold both pain and pleasure in one moment.

In these days of COVID infection, when family hugs are missing, and every touch could be a danger, I'm more likely to want to enhance sensation—to notice my fingers' soft paddling of the keyboard as I type, to turn my face deliberately to let the draft from the window play with my hair. I will savor the sensation of the cup and hot tea as they touch my lips. We are all starved of touch at a time when we most need comfort. We most value deliberate touch when we want to soothe people. We might pat a hand, or stroke it, or hug someone close if they're distressed.

So how do you soothe with writing? Not easy. To engage a reader is to put them under tension. Yet words can comfort, and many have found relief by reading—by revisiting the old favorites associated with more relaxed and comfortable times, by digging out the nostalgic copies of Dickens or *The House at Pooh Corner*. Reading can lessen anxiety by taking you to a fictional world far away from your current worries, and in fact a study by the University of Sussex measured the heart rate and muscle relaxation of volunteers and found that reading reduced stress by 68 percent in its case studies.

In the same way as the childhood game, reading allows a painful experience to be safe. Books encompass the sensations of pain and pleasure together and in the same moment. This moment, often experienced intimately and alone, is nevertheless a touchpoint where our common humanity meets, where we acknowledge that to be alive can be both painful and beautiful.

The Art of Reading with Your Ears

KATE NILES

Last September, my husband and I moved to Providence, Rhode Island, in part because it had a community boating center where we could rent a sailboat without owning one, and thus tack back and forth in a little section of Narragansett Bay. However, you had to pass a "challenge test"—which means being able to turn the boat and maintain a course. I, a lifelong Southwesterner, had no idea how to do such a thing.

Despite COVID, the Providence Community Boating Center offered sailing classes this summer, starting later than usual, but starting nonetheless. Not only would I learn to sail—something my husband had learned in childhood and loved—but I would get out of the house and spend time with other people. Hubby would run errands and pick me up after we were all done. The lessons on land took place around picnic tables tucked under the center's main building, built on stilts to withstand floods. I teamed up with a young couple from (of all places) Santa Fe, close by western standards to our old home in Durango, Colorado, and a place I have lived in the past. I chatted with my new friends about green chili and desert thunderstorms as we braced ourselves for interaction with an entirely new ecosystem. On a whiteboard, one of our young instructors explained wind direction, close haul, beam, reach, tacking, jibing, heeling—the language of the nautical world. The term "old dog new tricks" kept creeping into my middle-aged brain.

I was worrying about dyslexic right-left tiller maneuvers when someone asked how a person could gauge wind direction when they couldn't see a flag flapping. Our instructor, who was tan and wore white Crocs that set off a well-formed set of legs, said, "I know the wind is behind me when I feel it on the backs of my ears."

If I were twenty, I would have fallen in love right then and there. It was such a statement of presence, as if his ears were caressing breezes and the breezes caressing his ears. I have learned to consult cedar trees in times of distress and feel happiest when I sense how all of us are like aspens—rhizomes and thus one organism. But my gift is intuition, not sensation. I work as a psychotherapist, so if presented with a suicide crisis I am perfectly at home. But here in Rhode Island? On a hot Saturday morning at water's edge? Just as COVID has demanded I stare into a camera all day long to work with clients; just as the East is demanding different fabrics and routines than the West (wool, not fleece! quick-dry shirts, not cotton!); just as my husband and I are navigating a whole new world, I am being asked to work with my hands to hoist sails—and feel things with the backs of my ears.

Dog magic, I think. *Fox sense, horse knowledge, whale sonar.*

As we sail out on the bay—we Desert Rats in one sixteen-foot starter boat with a small jib, a manageable mainsail, and lightweight construction—it becomes apparent one of us has remembered more from childhood than he thought. "Pay attention to when the tiller catches the water," the male of our trio calls out. "You'll know to recenter.... See that flat place in the water? The wind dies there.... The sail will let you know when the wind is enough."

So much of sailing happens by feel; so much is listening, sensing, touching in strangely analytical ways. I am reminded of my stumbling attempts at knitting.

The move to Rhode Island has been about deepening a twenty-eight-year relationship. My husband and I raised a son, put an old dog down, and felt increasingly stuck in our beautiful but remote Colorado town. We spent at least two years checking out smaller cities to inhabit, seeking a sense of community, intellectual and artistic stimulation, the right natural climate to explore. Nobody, apparently, deliberately moves to Providence unless it's for work or college. This is somewhat of a mystery to me, since the city has pulled itself out of its postindustrial slump and offers myriad restaurants, lectures, music, art, parks, train rides to Boston or New York, and (for us) proximity to my in-laws' summer place forty-five minutes away. Still, for me to leave the West—site of a gut-wrenching childhood as well as deep salvation in immense landscapes—has been brutally disorienting. The other day, after talking with a friend in Colorado who told me it had finally rained, I broke into wracking sobs. I had a flash of standing in her weedy driveway, with a few purple asters making an appearance next to the sage, and the *smell* of those plants in that rain—the great relief of it—overpowered me.

Five months after moving into our apartment COVID hit, and our well-laid plans for concerts, trips, theater, and the like were put on hold. Late at night, with the back door open to our second-floor balcony, I often wondered how awful it would be to live alone, to not have the simple, animal necessity of my husband next to me. My son, a continent away in Washington State, terrifies me in his isolation, even as his introverted temperament makes certain aspects of this whole thing easier. He camps and fishes with a close friend, but he has not been hugged, shaken a hand, clapped a back, in months. I project all my own fears of such a state onto him. I have yearned to hug him as I did when he was four. He is twenty-two. We are in The Time of Letting Go, but this mother feels her bear-self wanting to sense fur on fur, that singular connection mothers have for their offspring if all goes well with their innate instinct to nurture. But I am not in Washington—I sleep in a second-floor apartment in Rhode Island that feels at times like a tree house, with its fledgling robins out back and a screeching blue jay. And now I am on a semireclaimed bay, learning to sail.

I do okay with the mainsail, less so with the jib and tiller. The three of us switch off tasks. When it's my turn at the tiller, I take it and sort of get it, though the first jibe—turning the boat with the wind behind you—is a near disaster because I try to recenter too quickly. The sail is behind me, and I find I should be listening for it, sensing its position, to time the tiller. Later, my husband will draw a boat in the dirt and explain that sailing alone is perhaps easier because you don't have communication issues. He'll reveal a neat trick of keeping the sail heeled in until just the right point and *then* jibing, because otherwise the whole thing can be a violent affair.

Nobody taught us that on this day—we are the only boat, for some reason, without an accompanying junior boatmaster. So we fumble along, for the most part doing okay—until the second jibe. This time my sail mate grows timid and doesn't let the sail out in time, just as I am going a might too hard with the tiller. And over we go.

The first thing you learn about capsizing, at least on a small boat with a convenient float atop its mast, is that it is not that bad. I am delighted to discover that my lifejacket works great, my sneakers do not weigh me down, and, looking toward shore, I realize quite happily that, if worse came to worst, I could just swim. If others know the body memory of sailing, I know swimming; I am still in possession of my varsity letter sweater from high school.

The water is pleasant on this hot day, and thanks to our land lessons we know what to do. The other two swim around to the centerboard, I drape myself over the down edge, and as the boat rights itself I scoop into it like a caught tuna. Meanwhile, the boating center skiff has come out, and the instructors are pleased with us: "That was a classic recovery."

We sail back to the dock for water and a bathroom break. We have been out for two and a half hours. My boat mates are eager to go back on the water, but I realize my brain has reached a saturation point. I feel computationally old and stand somewhat stupidly on the dock. The wind is coming at me, so my face feels it, not my ears. But at least I am paying attention to this fact.

I text my husband to come get me. I am well aware that the "challenge test" is not within reach for me today. My twenty-something would-be love interest says sure, come by any time after four on a weekday and we'll go out.

At sunset, in the dirt, I hear the scratch of the stick my husband uses to draw the boat and demonstrate jibing. We are at the family place in western Massachusetts, the trees set in their summer heaviness, dinner an hour away with masked and socially distanced loved ones. The Earth has gone quiet. It is a relief to be on somewhat familiar ground, though I am still in New England and far from my dry, sage-ridden flats with mountains looming. I hardly know what territory I'm in anymore, and my uprooting is mirrored by the nation's. *We* don't know what territory we are in anymore.

There are nights I lie awake at three a.m.—uncertain, disturbed. I should not read the news. *Stay present,* says my boat. *Feel the wind with the backs of your ears,* says my boat instructor. Or, as Gary Snyder wrote decades ago in his poem "For the Children," *Stay together / learn the flowers / go light.* I am beginning to see there is no other way.

Touched by the Soul

PHYLLIS M SKOY

Even after thirty-some years, I find myself wondering about Alice. Where does she live? How does she spend her days? Is there anyone she loves? Has she learned to love being touched?

Alice was my first child patient. She was born profoundly deaf and she progressed, by the age of seven, when I first met her, to becoming profoundly defiant. As a young and inexperienced psychotherapist, I agreed to work with Alice only in exchange for ensnaring the supervision of the medical director. He had all the experience and knowledge I lacked, and in my naiveté, I thought I'd gotten the best of bargains. As time proved, I actually had.

No one understood quite why Alice had to be so bad, but I always had the sense that there was purpose actively hatching in that intelligent brain. At the age of four, Alice had heart surgery. Her parents did not sign, and at that age, neither did Alice. She had no idea what was happening to her. According to Alice's mother, the four-year-old Alice walked in on her father viewing fellatio in a pornographic film. Once again, there was no explanation or communication. We were never able to determine whether or not anything else of this nature, or even something worse, had occurred.

Alice's play reflected these incidents in creative dramas that continued from session to session like an ongoing television series. Through the use of puppets, stuffed animals, miniature figures used for sand-tray therapy, and drawings, Alice revealed her life to me. In her created stories, Hermie the Hippo would have to be driven to the hospital in the middle of the night, ambulance siren wailing. She would use a letter opener to reenact the heart surgery on Hermie. In another ongoing scenario, she buried tiny rubber pigs in the sand tray. Before the end of the session, she slowly retrieved them one by one. This went on for weeks, until I interpreted to her that she feared I might become pregnant and leave her, as had occurred with a prior therapist. When she felt she had conveyed what she wished to impart to me in one set of dramas, she would seductively wind her fingers through her string blond hair and announce that we were going to play Uno in the next session. I came to learn that this signified the shift to a completely new series. All of these encounters took place in American Sign Language (ASL).

No matter how evocative her play became, I knew from Alice's history that physical contact with her was forbidden. Sometimes I would have one puppet hug another puppet who had undergone some form of distress in Alice's play enactments. I would sign to her that Pink Bear was hurt, and that Hermie the Hippo wanted to comfort him. Often, she would simply watch this interaction without comment, but there were other times when she would take Hermie the Hippo from me and give him a good beating. When I asked what Hermie the Hippo had done to deserve this treatment, she would laugh and sign that Hermie was bad. Further discussion on this topic was not to be pursued at the time. As I was being trained psychoanalytically, I simply waited. I believed that eventually Alice would reveal all that she needed me to know.

A year passed. I went on vacation to Italy. When I returned, her teacher joked that I was not allowed to have any more vacations. Alice had kicked her in a temper tantrum. Apparently, Alice's behavior had been improving to such a degree that the kick had been a shock to everyone.

Years passed. Alice and I created a photo book together of her birthdays, her play, her art. She made a colorful name drawing for my office door, so pleased with herself when we hung it there.

But as time went on, my talented and curious supervisor pressed me to reveal to Alice the hypothesis we had developed with regard to her bad behavior. It was really not that much of a hypothesis, as she had come right out and revealed the goal of her badness. She had looked me square in the eye and signed, "If I'm bad enough, I'll be bad like a boy. And then I will grow a penis." But I had hesitated to confront Alice with the impossibility of this belief. We were getting along so well. Why would I want to disrupt all the improvements she'd made by destroying her fantasy?

Why would I risk tumbling from the throne on which she'd placed me and turning her adoration into hatred? So more time passed. My supervisor pressed. I resisted, becoming almost as oppositional as Alice. But, of course, Alice was the smarter of the two of us, and she demanded of me what she knew she must have, the truth.

One day, shortly after Alice turned eleven, she burst into my office filled with what I assumed was intention. I sensed that there was something different in the air. She twirled around in her chair for several moments before facing me head-on and announcing, "If I'm bad, very, very bad, I will grow a penis."

This time, I didn't hesitate. I signed back to her, "No, no matter how bad you are, you won't ever be able to grow a penis." Now I know there are those today who might say I should have immediately educated her on transexual procedures and what might be available to her, but even in my premature stages of experience, and although it was the early eighties, that never would have occurred to me.

We sat and looked at one another. Several minutes passed. Alice signed, "Never? Even if I'm very bad?"

I did not back down, even though my heart was breaking for her. "Never," I signed.

Alice, who had never cried with me before, burst into tears. Her body shook. Her skinny arms embraced her tiny body. Head lowered, her legs pulled up under her, she sobbed.

You cannot imagine how hard it was for me to remain in my chair. I wanted to run to her, to hug her and to comfort her. Every muscle in my body tensed with restraint. I knew I could not contain myself for very long. I thought I might go crazy just sitting there for an hour. But after what seemed like an excruciating amount of time, something shifted in me that I knew had to be coming from her. I allowed myself to go with it. In my mind, Alice became four, the age of her various traumas. I pictured myself holding her, stroking her hair, massaging her back, hugging her close to me. I sent my soul out to soothe her.

I stayed with my reverie. She sobbed in hers. And yet, I must say, this was one of the most intimate hours I experienced in all my years of treatment.

No more words were exchanged between us that day. Alice was composed when she left. She simply signed, "I'll see you in two days." I could feel the change. She had passed through a great deal on her journey to maturity. We had not physically touched, but our minds had embraced to an extent that our bodies never would.

Some therapists think about touch a great deal. Others don't think that much about it at all. We are Americans, and we hug at random. When I visited China, one of my tour guides embraced me with a big smile. When I commented that I didn't find hugging to be so common among the Chinese, she laughed. "They teach us how to hug in tourism school. They say Americans love to hug, so we must learn to do it."

What I learned from Alice is how creative one can be in achieving human intimacy. I never asked Alice if she felt my embraces that day, and she never told me. Whatever I transmitted to her, she knew she was being held and heard in a way she had not known prior to these moments. This "touch" from the soul had the power to change us both.

Where It Happens

SARAH MOON

When coronavirus first hit, you could almost hear the doors slamming shut, slowly at first, and then so rapidly we were spinning. It began with the public doors of the sports arenas, theaters, and restaurants, and later became the doors of your friends, your extended family. Pretty soon, the only door left open was your own.

Schools went virtual. Restaurants shifted to takeout. Sports organizations regrouped. But most theaters simply waited, dark. The sickness of Broadway actor Nick Cordero, who passed away in July 2020, seemed like a metonymy for the whole industry. But not only were Broadway shows shut down, every tiny theater in America was shuttered.

In January 2020, I had launched a food-centered community performance project called Write Your Roots. We were set to perform a set of seven original monologues at a small theater in Pawtucket, Rhode Island. For the closing, the performers would sit around a dining table to read the poem "Perhaps the World Ends Here" by Joy Harjo. There would be an audience of some fifty to sixty people sitting close together, knees brushing knees, shoulders brushing shoulders, breath mingling with breath. But in the week leading up to that date, such proximity began to seem unwise, and by the end of the week, it was officially forbidden. We postponed the show indefinitely.

This loss made me think even more about a concept with which I was already obsessed: liveness. In the wake of our coronavirus isolation, it's a subject many have been examining from a new perspective. What is it that we lose when we are not and cannot be together in person?

For me, the answer is a kind of spiritual touch, a touch that I know happens when people are together in the same room. Have you sat in the dark, watching and listening to a singer, and cried? Have you been a performer onstage and felt the audience's attention drawing you out like the tide? There is, on the part of both the audience member and the performer, an invisible energy generated through live performance, an energy that I believe cannot be fully translated through a screen and speakers.

For some, this magic I take as reality is highly suspect. In the digital age, they feel, you should submit to the screen and not wax on about some immeasurable energy conveyed through live performance. But if this magical energy can't be proven through scientific measurement, perhaps its realness is confirmed by the difference in what people will spend for it. People will pay three hundred dollars to see *Hamilton* on Broadway, but they would not likely spend more than thirty dollars to watch it on Disney+.

I can trace my own obsession with the powerful touch of live performance back to high school. Led by an intrepid veteran director, my high school theater department produced *Evita* my freshman year, and it was perhaps the luckiest thing that ever happened to me. I was only fourteen, and timid at that, so I was cast in a chorus role. But two senior powerhouses, Ben Sheaffer and Kate Baldwin, were cast as Che Guevara and Eva Perón. Both actors went on to star on Broadway.

Though I loved singing and acting in that show, I really loved watching Ben and Kate. Their energy was awe-inspiring as they hit those high notes or delivered a line from the gut, laced with sarcasm. *Evita* was the greatest thrill of my young life.

I didn't physically touch either actor at any point in the play, and yet I was deeply, permanently touched by their performances. And I never could have been touched that way watching them on video, even if it were live. I might have been entranced, delighted, entertained. But not touched in the way that I was.

The great performer conjures a kind of force field that an audience member is invited into, and, if they enter, an energy is shared and exchanged. You walk out of the theater with some residue of that energy hanging about you like a starry cloud. Sometimes you carry it as far as your pillow and it stays with you in your dreams. Sometimes you carry it with you for the rest of your life.

Of the Italian actress Eleonora Duse, George Bernard Shaw wrote in a review, "With a tremor of the lip, which you feel rather than see, and which lasts half an instant, [she] touches you straight on the very heart." When Shaw wrote those words, TV and film did not exist. There was no way to experience an actor's talent other than to watch her on stage. But even today, with our advanced media technologies, we clamor for the live experience. Performance studies scholar Philip Auslander notes in his book *Liveness* that the Walt Disney Company has a division specifically devoted to repurposing its films into live performances. He also cites a 2007 Broadway revival of *Grease* in which the cast was decided through the reality TV show *Grease: You're the One That I Want*, noting how the fact that the TV show would eventually become a live performance made it more special.

Live performance is not an underdog on the brink of relevance but rather exists and will always exist in relationship with mediatized culture. As Auslander points out, even the corporate entertainment giants acknowledge there is still a sociocultural value attached to live, in-person events.

In response to a 2014 post on *The New York Times* Learning Network Blog titled "Does Live Theater Offer Something You Just Can't Get Watching Movies or TV?," people replied affirmatively in the comments section using words such as "magic," "amazement," "uncertainty," "thrill," and "appreciate." One commenter wrote, "It's where you can feel the vibration of the actor's voice and hear their hoarse and raw voices."

Unlike actors seen on the screen, actors that we watch onstage more obviously display their humanity. Their faces have sweat on them, their voices sometimes crack. We can see and feel that they are just like us, flesh and blood. Yet their performances amaze us. We watch them, understanding the energy it must take for them to give what they are giving. My favorite moment of any great show is the curtain call. In the curtain call, all together, we acknowledge what the performers have given us. We honor them by clapping, maybe standing and cheering, and they beam back at us. You never get to experience that at the end of the movie. Those actors are far away, oblivious to their audience.

Several theaters have worked valiantly to mount shows for Zoom audiences. I think this is important. It allows the actors to keep working their muscles, and if it can't offer shared space, it does at least offer shared time.

The tone of the voice, the look in the eye, can move us in this context too. And the performers can hear us clapping at the end.

But we still ache for what is missing, the electricity of shared air.

Now shared air represents disease. Even if our bodies don't touch, the virus that comes from one of our bodies could touch another and make them ill. Despite the proximity we long for, we can't risk it.

I live with two young children, my husband, a cat, and a dog. I have been lucky to regularly experience the pleasure of physical touch in this time. But I haven't experienced that feeling of being touched through performance. It sits outside the realm of possibility, suspended indefinitely. In the meantime, we have opted to create a video of the Write Your Roots monologues.

One day, the theaters will reopen their doors. I cannot wait for that first curtain call, when we'll applaud not only for the performance but for the sheer happiness of being there together again.

Touch Typing

by Paul Singer

I am not, by any measure, a touch-typist.

I whack away at these old manual type-
writers -- this one a 1936 Corona portable
-- exactly as I have since I was a child:
four fingers pecking away one key at a
time. Even though I write for a living,
I really can't type. It is the enduring
curse of being the Last Guy in America to
finish college without ever using a
personal computer.

But this affliction of being more at
ease in a mechanical environment than a
digital one has turned out to have an
unexpected side benefit: It is through
typing that I touch people.

This was true before the pandemic, but
it became urgently more true once we all
got shut away from each other.

I have always kept a manual typewriter
at the office, mostly for the purpose of
leaving notes for my colleagues. Rather
than send an e-mail six desks away saying
"check out this New York Times story
about bacon," I am much more likely to
walk the print version over to my co-
worker's cubicle with a little typed
note saying, "Check out the bacon story.
Thought of you."

When I joined my new newsroom in Boston
a few years ago, I brought with me a
typewriter and a habit of delivering
tiny epistles.

When a colleague has a good story pub-

lished or broadcast, I roll a Post-It
into the platen and type a few words of
encouragement -- "Liked the whale story!
(But maybe shoulda interviewed a dolphin
for rebuttal?").

I discovered that unlike a congratula-
tory email or a shout-out in a staff
meeting, these little notes have permanence.
People keep them. Stick them to their
cubicle walls. One colleague responded with
glee when I brought a Post-It to her desk.
"I was hoping I would get a Singer note
for that story! Yay!"

The pandemic stole this small joy from us.

I have tried a few times since the quaran-
tine to type up a congratulatory Post-It for
a co-worker and then take a picture of it
and text it to them... but it just isn't
the same. There is something about the
feel of the letters pressed into the paper
and the ability to hold in your hand an
object that was machine-made, but just
for you. It touches people in a way that
a text or email never will.

So COVID stole from me this ability to
touch my colleagues in a simple but lasting
way that has helped knit our work-family
together.

But there is also another side to this
page.

Quarantine kept me home most evenings,
and being home has often sent me to the
typewriter, where I will sit with a glass
of wine and some good music and clank out
a letter to an old friend.

These things, little objects of my

affection, are generally two or three page
mutterings on any subject; meandering
little monologues on a moment of time. But
they seem to have an out-sized impact when
they arrive. It is so rare that people
receive a hand-made anything in the mail
these days, and there appears to be a
magical moment when one discovers among
the bills, solicitations and catalogues
an actual #10 envelope with an actual
first-class stamp and a little smudged
typewriter ink on the front.

Ironically, the first reaction of most
of my friends is to pick up some electronic
device and send me a text or email to say,
"WOW, I got an ACTUAL letter..."

Very very few of them type a letter back.
But almost all of them respond in some
thoughtful, heartfelt way.
And I belive the typewriter is part of
the reason for that.

There is something about a dispatch from
a prior century that seems to require
response and recognition. When your grand-
father calls, you answer. And when your
grand-father's technology reaches out, you
afford it the same respect.

But the machine is only part of the story.
The other part is about time.

Time together is the thing we have lost
most to this horrible pandemic. But the
time I spend banging out a letter on an old
manual typewriter is time spent thinking
of you. The time you spend reading that
missive is time spent thinking about what
we mean to each other. When you sit down
to reply, you expand the circumference
of this bubble we are creating around

ourselves, a space we clear in our clutter of thoughts just for each other. It allows us a little time together, even at this great, infected distance.

The typewriter has thus become a time machine. It carries us back together to the "before" days, when we had time to spend together. And time together is the thing we have been longing for.

<u>This</u> is touch typing.

touch delayed

Reflections of a Hologram

ROBERT ROOT

In this time of pandemic, I avoid intermingling with others. I keep my distance from strangers and, with exceptions, from everyone I know. My wife and I are solidly senior, and Wisconsin's aggressive ragweed has heightened her asthma, so we maintain a low profile in hopes the coronavirus won't notice us. We shop intermittently and choose curbside pickup whenever possible. We roll the windows up, put on our masks, open the trunk from the dashboard, hear someone deposit our purchases, and then wave and yell "Thank you!" to workers we might never recognize unmasked. We enter only familiar stores that demand masking and relentlessly smear on hand sanitizer as if it's what we always do when we get in the car. We walk in the street to avoid people on the sidewalk, often mumbling a hello and assuming we're all smiling encouragingly under our masks. By now, too many months into pandemic living, we need to research what day of the week it is, wonder if it's the same month or a new one. I have the recurring sense of having lived through this day not a week ago but yesterday, and I'm not always certain what day will follow this one. All days are the same; why give them individual names?

I often wake up alone in bed—my wife gets up earlier, but I resist rising, force myself to admit I'm awake only when I start seething about some political travesty instead of trying to remember what happened in the busy dream that dissipated with morning light. Less often, I wonder what I should do after making the bed, turning on my laptop in the study, and going downstairs to make coffee and empty the dishwasher, but when I arrive at my desk, I first work on easy online crossword puzzles and jigsaws, then I check the weather. Eventually I open my email, although, except for Facebook notices of someone's birthday, I'm unlikely to have any email requiring replies. It's often a challenge to recall something I might have intended to do. I'm now adept at not thinking as much as possible. With my wife working in another room until we meet for breakfast, it's quiet in the condo.

Too often, when I go into the bathroom, I wonder who I'm looking at in the mirror. Oh, I know who he is, but I don't know what he's doing—what proves his existence. He could be a hologram—he seems three-dimensional, visible from several different angles—but neither he nor I seem to occupy real physical space. I face him, sometimes gesture rudely at him, as he does to me. I'm aware of my own actual existence only through pains in the small of my back or wrists or knees from sitting at my desk and operating my laptop for too long. If my mirror image were to ask me what I touch to prove my existence in my world, I would have to list those things. Those things and the sheets, blanket, bedspread, and pillows when I made the bed, the coffee filter and coffee grounds and buttons on the coffee maker and the thermal coffee cup, the dishes in the dishwasher and the kitchen cabinet doors and drawers, all these my physical connection with my world, how I perform my existence. In the bathroom, after shaving and brushing my teeth, I gaze again at the figure in the mirror. He is a hologram once more, and I am again out of touch with any certainty about my existence.

Out of touch. It's the negative of being *in* touch, of getting *in* touch, of keeping *in* touch. "Let's stay in touch," someone says after a meeting or conversation, or "I'll be out of touch until Monday," someone advises. "Touch" here is communication, a phone call or an email, a "text message" or something similarly remote. Nearly two decades ago I left a college teaching job and later a subsequent online mentoring job and have been *out of* touch with virtually everyone I taught with and all but a few people I taught. Some stay *in* touch haphazardly online, letting anyone who has "friended" them see photographs of their children, their families, their pets; informing them of birthdays, anniversaries, marriages, promotions, deaths; updating their "profile pictures" to highlight changes in hairstyles, ages, attitudes. I sometimes "like" some of their posts, if I think my thumbs-up won't be intrusive. To avoid appearing polite but insincere, I seldom comment or repeat the good wishes or commiserations of others. Am I really staying *in* touch through those "likes" and emojis and stock phrases? Would anyone notice if I didn't respond at all? Responses seem like those golden records on the *Voyager* spacecrafts, messages intended for extraterrestrial beings, any reply entirely unanticipated and only subconsciously hoped for.

I've experienced some current ways of keeping in touch online. Before the pandemic I'd been on Skype with students, the ones needing face-to-face conversation or advice. I've sometimes been on Zoom: as a silent audience member for a discussion of Thoreau, as a committee member for a local group, as part of a family book club our daughter initiated (she's since switched to Google Hangouts). Over months of isolation, we've connected through FaceTime to the kids in Florida and the kid in California and even, during a non-COVID illness in their family, the kids here in Wisconsin. I occasionally consider FaceTime-ing my wife in the next room, to reinforce each other about whatever we are or aren't doing. Such communication has challenges: people who haven't been doing anything don't have much to share about their activities, and people who have been doing things—a few of our gang still have day jobs, even if they often work from home—tend not to be specific about the taxes the accountant is working on, the projects the engineer is overseeing, the scripts the screenwriter is supervising. Worse, screen images often emphasize the silences, the uncertainties about what to say. *"What's new?" "Nothing much. What's new with you?" "Well, same ol' same ol.'"* One of us looks out a window, another looks at their keyboard, another looks at a wall. Occasionally some repartee gets going; usually we're simply reassured that we're still where we usually are—that we're still alive. We can claim to have been *in touch*, but after we end the call, we are, most often, sharply aware of how long it's been since we actually *touched* any of them. The persistent sense of distance sometimes makes me, well, touchy, as if we were all simply computer animations, only holograms on one another's computer screens, incapable of actual contact, of physical touch.

Touch. Among *Merriam-Webster's* thirty-four slightly different definitions of "touch"—as a transitive verb, an intransitive verb, and a noun, some with further subdivisions—many are metaphors for the intangible ("a touch of fever," "the touch of a master"), but some refer to the concrete and scientific ("the special sense by which pressure or traction exerted on the skin or mucous membrane is perceived," "a specified sensation that arises in response to stimulation of the tactile receptors"). I'd searched for an antonym of "hologram" and couldn't find one, but I found references to what a hologram was *not*, emphasizing the inability of a hologram or a computer animated figure to touch, to feel, to experience physical, tactile contact. A hologram embodies the absence of touch, that connection between people that makes them feel like living human beings occupying the same physical space rather than simply sharing the same electronic airwaves that simultaneously project one another's digital images. *Let's keep in touch as long as we make sure we don't actually touch.* I am no longer a father, father-in-law, grandfather—I am merely a hologrampa, as remote from all of my family as from the self who glares back at me in the bathroom mirror.

Occasionally, once a week or so, we meet our daughter, son-in-law, and grandchildren for a socially distanced dinner in their backyard. Six months ago, as we did each time we got together, we would all hug one another saying hello again and hug one another saying goodbye. It's a habit I picked up from my wife's family, not a common one in my background before our marriage, except with my own children. When our daughters married, the hugging continued, comfortably, with their husbands and then with our grandchildren. Now, with all of us housebound, we no longer embrace one another in Wisconsin, won't embrace if we finally get to Florida once more, can't determine when we'll embrace our son in California again. We gain something by the touch of those we love that being *in touch* in any other way doesn't offer.

Within minutes of your child's birth, touch expands your sense of your existence: the first time you brush the flesh of a naked newborn, the warmth of that small body in your arms, the taste of that forehead on your lips. You hold and caress that child thinking you offer reassurance, comfort, love, and may not realize at first what you receive from the child you touch, an unspoken awareness that your universe is simultaneously larger and more compressed than it was just moments before. The intense, inarticulate immediacy of love is expressed most intimately through touch and in a family broadens and deepens across time. That infant you adored instantaneously becomes the toddler who stumbles laughing into your arms, the child who falls asleep in your lap as you read another book aloud, the new cyclist finding balance from your guiding hand, and so on across the years. In time your children are adults bringing new life into the world of their own, and that aching cycle of touch begins anew, enriched by its links to those grandchildren's parents. When you embrace the grandson already grown taller than you, the grand-daughter shyly pleased about her driving license, you embrace again all the stages of their lives, all the stages of their parents' lives, perhaps the stages of your own life. Had you even suspected that such breadth, such depth, such intensity of love could express itself through something so simple as touch? It can. It does.

One way to realize the power of simple touch is be deprived of its possibility by becoming—no matter how affectionate, how cheerful, how supportive, how sincere—someone who can be *in touch* only as a hologram. Our Florida daughter joked about looking forward to sharing air hugs when we meet again, hoping that holograms can cuddle. But such air hugs would simply pass through one another, at best provide an imaginary intimacy; instead of enriching family connection by touch, they may only heighten our sense of living our lives as holograms.

Vestigial Imprint

ANNE CASEY

How I searched for you everywhere—
fingers buried in the folds
of your nightdress,
pressed to lips,
a trace of you surviving
the unintended
washing.

How I catch you sometimes
in my son's half
-smile, his sideways glance;
how he is unaware
of you there

between us in a hug,
my in-breath when I kiss
his head.

How he wriggled
from my lap—knees
grazing the polished boards
as four days before
we blew out
his first candles
around your bedside.

How unconsciously I called
your name, embraced
your lingering
warmth, waves crashing
over and over
below us—the weight
of water
pounding rock

those dark hours as your hand froze
to ice in mine, how still
I search for you
in midnight skies,
eyes cast upwards
palms cupped,
ready to catch

the smallest trace.

Wish You Were Here

NICOLE HARDY

The day after the WHO declared COVID-19 a global pandemic, I discovered I've been living on the site of a former sanatorium. I'd heard rumors since I first moved into my condo in 2005—a roomy one-bedroom right on the beach just south of the Fauntleroy ferry that I could never afford in today's market. People said it was once a mental institution, or a place for alcoholics to dry out. One neighbor swears that in the '40s two dead bodies floated past one morning when he was skipping stones at the beach with a friend. *They came from up there,* he said, meaning my place. I never knew what to believe until I got an email from Jim—head of our emergency preparedness committee:

For those of you "self-quarantining" there is good news. We are naturally isolated, and this "splendid isolation" includes views which are always interesting and often spectacular. As many of you already know, this was once a kind of quarantine zone. The Laurel Beach Sanatorium for tuberculosis victims. There was a reason they chose this location.

"It reads like an ad for the world's creepiest tourist destination," I joked online. That was three weeks ago, when quarantine was still mostly an abstraction.

"Quarantinis" had just become a thing.

Tone-deaf as it was, I found Jim's email comforting. In the early 1900s—when TB was the leading cause of death in Seattle—isolation, fresh air, good food, and rest was the only treatment. There was nothing to do but ride it out. I can see how Jim drew the parallel between then and now. And at the time, I figured I knew how to do this: I've worked from home for years; I've always been single; and normally I love living alone.

There was no way to know how quickly a pandemic could turn welcome solitude into crushing isolation.

At the beginning, social distancing didn't seem so bad. I could still date, according to two of three experts interviewed for the *Atlantic*. All we had to do was wash our hands, not be symptomatic, and sit apart from other people. "Totally worth risking death," my most recent said at the bar at Underbelly, leaning in to kiss me. Now that move seems both reckless and stupid.

That was when I could still walk with a friend (six feet apart), worrying aloud about my job, my mortgage, and my mom, who just turned seventy-two, has asthma and a history of pneumonia, lives eleven miles from the Life Care Center of Kirkland—Washington's epicenter—and watches only Fox News. The people she trusts were still calling the pandemic a hoax when more than eighty thousand people had fallen ill in China, more than three thousand had died, and infections were dotting the globe.

That was before #stayhomestaysafe, which erased my income and all human contact; when a friend could still drop by and edit proofs of a book on its way to publication while ten feet away I prepped for lockdown: quinoa, lentils, white bean soup, turkey chili, pumpkin muffins—anything that'd fill my freezer, which held exactly two ice trays, one box of baking soda, and a bag of compost. We'd both already begun to feel the unfamiliar, pressing need to have another heartbeat in the room.

It's now been sixty-six days since I've touched, or been touched by, any living thing, and we're just getting started. Alone in this pandemic, I feel anxious and fragile—two things I can't stand. Loneliness lives in my body now. It's a constant ache down my spine, across my shoulders and chest, up the tendons in my neck. Sometimes I sleep horizontally, my back pressed against the headboard—trying to fool my body into the feeling of being held.

My mom called today. She keeps inviting me to watch movies; I keep telling her about Iceland—how they tested basically everyone and discovered that a huge percentage of infected people are asymptomatic.

"I'd hate to be the one to murder you," I said, and we both laughed until she started coughing.

"But I miss you," she said.

I don't let myself think about the scenario in which I've already seen her for the last time. Or the one in which that kiss at that bar was the last kiss of my life. Instead, I binge on TV so fictional I can't relate. First it was *Breaking Bad*, now it's *Better Call Saul*. My plan worked perfectly until yesterday, when in some poignant scene Kim touched Jimmy's face. Neither said anything. She sensed his sadness and brushed her fingers against his cheek. That gesture gutted me. I broke down sobbing, only partly because what if I've already been touched for the last time by someone who loves me.

Shame kicked in almost immediately, because who am I to be sad when so many people are in literal, mortal danger? When so many people have it so much worse. Sure, loneliness can also kill people—but that's not where I am, and that's not today. To put my problems in perspective, I keep pulling up a *Reductress* story with the headline: "'It's Sort of Like Being in Prison,' Says Woman Eating Yogurt in Bed Who Also Has Voting Rights."

Perspective is everything.

Shame can work like a pep talk.

Most days, between TV binges and apocalyptic hailstorms, I walk the rocky beach in front of my condo, thinking that maybe what's connecting all of us right now is that everyone's feeling some version of powerless, overwhelmed, alone, and terrified. It's a strange way to be bound.

Out on the water's edge, I think about the patients quarantined in 1921. I imagine they woke up like I do: to a view like a postcard and the relentless ache of *wish you were here*. I picture them drinking coffee, buttering toast, also planning their days around walks at low tide. They stroll under the ferry dock not yet built, through Lincoln Park, which doesn't exist. We're all here, a century apart, breathing the same salt air. Putting our faith in the same simple, painful prescription. Wondering how long it'll take for good food, rest, and social distance to open a door to a room in a house filled with all the people who feel like home.

Common Ground

MAGDALENA BALL

Moss catches
between my fingers
the rough blindness of touch

every morning
after checking the worsening stats
I lean forward, ready to fall
find ground.

From this vantage
I make myself smaller
though I'm already minuscule
a deadly vector, a virus.

Keep your hands to yourself
keep (above all else) clean
miasmas are everywhere
death incubates in everything.

Alone with rock lilies and boulders
day and night are no longer binaries
not split into this and that
you and me
(with our sad state of affairs)
past and future

bleeding into sensation
in undifferentiated present
the sky darkens, opens, changes.

The risk is real, fabricated
in milky scars on my body
written in squid ink
beneath the sub-dermal layer of skin
a self-replicating tattoo
you'll never view
without contact.

Down here life isn't only
what you can taste
metallic and sweet
coined in hellish mints
traded for a few more hours
another step upward
another rung.

There is only so much time
(time as illusory, pliant, *relative*)
to taste, feel, breathe in
slowly, decadently
while breath is still a thing

I lean into this space
body to body
as organism
ontological roots
ravaged hands on
common earth.

A Personal History of Touch

DONNA BAIER STEIN

Touch has a Memory
—John Keats

This is a story of touch, both the presence and absence of it. This moment, nearly seven months into the worrisome spread of COVID-19, is a good place to begin.

Because I live alone, my dog, an eight-year-old Boston terrier named Sonny, has quite literally become my touchstone. I crave the warmth of his small body. My own body leans hungrily into his, intuitively knowing another heart beats beneath his brindle-and-white fur. That other beating heart is like a magnet, and I recall a remarkable passage in Sara Gruen's novel *Water for Elephants*:

"Afterward she lies nestled against me, her hair tickling my face. I stroke her lightly, memorizing her body. I want her to melt into me, like butter on toast. I want to absorb her and walk around for the rest of my days with her encased in my skin."

Like butter on toast. Encased in my skin. Ah life, how we so deeply long to connect to you!

The two of us, my dog and I, live in the large home I bought after my divorce. This house was once filled with my two children and my two parents and an earlier dog, a gentle golden retriever named Jake. There was plenty of touch in those years. There was plenty of touch in my marriage. And I've always been fortunate in the friendship of women and the reassuring hugs we offer one another.

But even hugs from friends have stopped with the risk of the virus, though one writer friend who visited last week offered me a hug as she left, and I gratefully accepted. Counting that hug, and hugs from my grown children when they have visited, I've been touched by a human being less than a dozen times in seven months. Not good!

I also cancelled the weekly massages I'd treated myself to for years. I now realize how vital they were to feeling a secure physical presence in the world.

I didn't grow up surrounded by touch. In fact, my parents were not at all physically demonstrative. Several decades ago, I was in a spiritual healing school when the teacher said, "You weren't hugged as a child, were you, Donna?" The words shocked me, but I knew they were true. I could not remember being hugged by my parents as a child, though we certainly hugged each other as adults, probably at my instigation. Despite the lack of childhood hugs, I knew and know they adored me. And it was only in the last year of my mother's life I learned a secret that may have led to her physical withdrawal.

I remember my momma rubbing Vicks VapoRub on my chest if I was sick, and the trips to the library we made, and the stories we wrote together. As an only child, I was the apple of my parents' eyes. But I very rarely saw my parents hug or kiss. In high school, I couldn't imagine they ever had sex though they obviously did once since I'm here. I believe my father might have wanted to be more physically demonstrative, but mom was obviously uncomfortable with anything more than an occasional peck on the cheek. I sometimes wondered if she'd been sexually abused, but she insisted she had not. However, the story she told me as we sat at my kitchen table in her ninety-fifth year, while not about an actual rape, says otherwise.

When my mother, a Christian, married my father, who had been raised in an Orthodox Jewish home, she converted to Judaism for three years. Part of her conversion included going to the *mikvah*, the ritual bath. What she told me about her experience there shocked me.

She said that she was not given any cloth covering to wear and no woman aide accompanied her into the water. Instead, three bearded rabbis peered at her through the windows as she stepped naked into the bath. It broke, and breaks, my heart to imagine my thin, sweet mother so flagrantly violated, not by touch but by sight. That too is abuse. I am so angry that it happened and so sad she carried that story inside her without ever telling a soul, not even my father.

My guess is that the violation she experienced rippled down to my own anxiety around touch and sexuality. I was a very late bloomer, losing my virginity in college, thanks in large part to marijuana. A series of sexual relationships after that were, for the most part, great. I loved sex.

My former husband and his parents were big huggers. And he loved sex too. I adored making love with him, feeling stimulated, seen, and adored. But then I got sidetracked caring for children who were occasionally challenging and learning of my husband's affair when my son was two. I pulled away emotionally and physically, felt a fear and lack of trust I had not felt before with him. Still, we stayed married and continued having sex, sometimes wonderful and sometimes not.

When I finally left the marriage in my midfifties, I didn't realize how much I would miss his hugs and lovemaking.

Since that divorce, I set about creating a single life filled with wonderful friends, writing, publishing, children, and caring for my aging parents.

Now, after both my parents have died, and my children are grown and flown, the absence of touch looms large.

In everyday life now midpandemic, my interactions with my dog Sonny are simple moments. At night we position ourselves in bed so his warm back touches mine, or we do a modified spoon, my arm loosely above his head. The first months after my divorce I longed for the feel of my husband's body in bed. We'd spent thirty years together, and the side of the bed where he once slept was a gaping chasm. I piled pillows there, hugging them. Sonny is more independent-minded than those pillows, and sometimes during the night he'll wander to a corner of the mattress, but he inevitably returns for physical contact he must enjoy as much as I do.

So often we take touch for granted. And yet its presence in our lives—through a hug, a kiss, a pat on the back, full-on lovemaking—brings multiple benefits. Science has proven that touch releases the "feel-good" hormone oxytocin, activates the vagus nerve, and boosts our immune system.

But to touch inappropriately can take life away. I firmly believe my mother was traumatized by that violation at the ritual bath. I've been thinking about this recently as I realize how touch-starved I am and how I sometimes feel my body shifting into a wary defensive presence in the world rather than an open-hearted, loving one.

I've been told that crossing my hands against my chest and gently pushing on my heart can also release that feel-good hormone, oxytocin. So I do that. I swim and do yoga and Jin Shin Jyutsu self-care practices. I even bought a new vibrator, and, during the writing of this essay, booked myself a massage.

Because it's become really clear to me how much we all need to be embraced with the touch of our loved ones, a friend, our dear and eager-to-love pets, or even with our own arms.

Michelangelo said, "To touch can be to give life." Picture the ceiling of the Sistine Chapel. Adam's index finger reaching out for but not quite touching God's finger. Even in the absence of physical touch, it is perhaps that internal longing that crosses any imaginary barrier of separation that reminds us of our continued connection to all that is.

tumultuous touch

BACK

PAULA COOMER

> To be alive is to be beaten, broken, demolished, and to be beaten,
> broken, demolished is to embody the purest form of beauty.
> — Lance Olsen, *My Red Heaven*

The sobs felt like granite boulders and my shoulders the mountain trying to shed them. This was new—the massage table, my face embedded into a donut-shaped cushion (or a hemorrhoid pillow, as I think about it now). The woman started gently, asking permission to touch me, beginning to work the almond oil into my skin. Never had another female touched me this way. Only once or twice had men whose ultimate goal was to reach the space between my legs.

When she began in earnest, going deep into the trapezius muscle at the base of my left shoulder blade, the first boulder broke loose. The phrase floated through whatever I was feeling: "She was racked with sobs."

The human back is a powerful machine, capable of carrying the weight of worlds. The weight of a life. Fifty tons? A hundred? A thousand? Imagine that weight in gravel, in boulders. A back is also a place to receive lashings—with a switch, a leather belt, a hairbrush, a mother's hand. To be beaten as a child is to live in terror, but to be beaten as an infant is not to know the difference between terror and love, fear and living. If you are often and with some regularity struck, you learn to arch against it, into it, to lessen, if only by self-distraction, the impact, and, hopefully, the pain. In the process you also develop an extraordinarily strong back, muscled from the exertion, one that can bear the burdens of generations.

My back has served me well, held me up like a sail through some pretty tough shit. I've often thought about myself in that way, my life as a thing set aloft for the sake of keeping the vessel of me afloat.

In my thirties and forties, weightlifting became a great passion. I wanted the strength to bear my second divorce, to raise my children alone. I would rather spend my hours in the weight room over anything else, escaping into my own body and my own limits and abilities. My sons, as a result, were raised in the gym childcare room, beginning at ages six and nine, spending many a bored hour watching TV, waiting for me to extend and retract muscles, pushing and pulling against dumbbells, iron plates, and resistance machines. Thirty-pound lat pulls per arm, twenty at a time for five reps, building those trapezius muscles into widening the V of my back, making it more pronounced and my shape less feminine. Lying against the bench with a hundred pounds on a twenty-five-pound bar, pushing me further into the padded bench, the touch not human but as much as I could stand at the time, unless it was the touch of a stranger seeking my deeper recesses. The bench was its own form of touch therapy or acupressure, working the nerves at the surface of my skin from the muscle side out.

My physician said to me, "I've never seen a back like this on a woman."

So, power. The power I needed and craved.

Try squat-lifting 265 pounds on a Smith Machine, and you'll understand that my back was capable of lifting an entire large male human being.

To what end, ultimately, I don't know. I still couldn't look my ex-husband in the eye, and he still treated me like a dog-poop baggie, filling me with shit about how worthless I was.

Which was good exercise and preparation because when life fell apart again and again, I had to pick myself up again and again. When you only know terror and fear, you recreate terror and fear over and over until you learn how not to. Only a strong back will carry you through.

Still, at thirty-five, I did not know the feeling of a loving touch, not to the back, the thigh, the soul, unless you count those primal moments when I nursed my sons, their lips full of love for the sustenance I provided, me rubbing their backs to soothe them in the middle of the night, them rewarding my motions with snuggles and coos.

In 1993, a year and a half after my divorce from my jackass of a second husband, I met a man. He, too, possessed a marvelous back—all the men I fell for had wide, burl-muscled backs.

Let's call this one Ricky. Moderately brilliant, good-looking, an urban-dweller, much more sophisticated than I, an innovative poet, songwriter, and musician, and a hedonistic drunk. He was the only man I'd met to that point who understood the full sensory range of the body. But he didn't use that knowledge on me, instead, craving it himself, manipulated me into providing certain services for him. I gave him long rubdowns, my one goal to communicate through his back and spine my desire to heal him of his anxiety, his depression, what he suffered from having been given up for adoption at birth, and from alcoholism. If I did a sufficient job for him, he might love me enough to render the same healing touch back to me. As the mother of two young boys, and the sole public health nurse for an entire Indian reservation, how did I have time for this? I let him convince me that my sons were causing him anxiety, and that was making him drink, therefore they needed to go live with their father.

Look, I'm not stupid. Of course, my sons had both been in counseling after the divorce, and I tried to help them adjust, but I was more consumed by the loss of partnership than I was concerned with them and their needs. Even my bad marriages came with tepid hugs and rotten sex, but still, I could count on the feeling of skin on skin. At least nobody was hitting me. I wanted, needed a kind hand on my flesh like it was medicine. Strangers could hold me under the sheets, I learned, same as people I was married to. I quickly found that any man could be seduced.

Seduction is the art of implying an outcome. I don't want to say I was good at it, but good enough for the kind of failed artist/alcoholic types I attracted. That's not to malign my fellow humans who have alcohol addiction. I'm saying people with alcohol addiction are not right *for me*. Eventually, I understood that I did myself no good by running out West and away from the people in my family with various addictions—which ranged from the bodies of tender, young girls to alcohol to drugs. Those very same addictions kept catching up to me anyway in the form of men. I might as well have stayed home in Indiana and fought face-to-face with my family's demons for the right to be myself.

To be an infant, alternately fussed over and spanked, skin on skin. *Spare the rod and spoil the child.* Mom, I try to imagine this, how you were, what my life felt like then. The first time you hit me must have left me in shock. Surely, I didn't stop crying, nor did your swats quench my needs. You couldn't have understood that, though, could you? Knowing your child-care ethics now, having watched you babysit for other children over the latter decade of my school years, I'm guessing you slapped my butt and legs and left me alone in the dark rooms of the basement that served as our house, listening to the scrape of pines against the outside wall. You left me alone to cry and suffer my unmet need in a womb of cement. There, at the fragile age of one month, two months, three, I learned no help was coming. No sustenance, no loving touch.

Hold the child and spoil the child. You read this in Dr. Spock's *Baby and Child Care.* You listened to the words of a white man over those of your Cherokee grandmother, the midwife. You've told me this. You wanted to bring me up according to the latest science: don't hold the baby unnec-essarily; prop the bottle to feed so she doesn't equate food with comfort (fat lot of good *that* did); breastfeeding is old-fashioned. Taking in bot-tles of cow's milk straight from the teats my father milked, albeit laced with dark Karo syrup—lord only knows why—I effectively suckled a cow rather than my own mother.

Two summers ago, my youngest son broke his back. He's something of a construction maniac, skills inherited from my master carpenter father, who could make anything from anything, who could build a car from parts just as easily as he could build a house or a high-rise building. He was trying to load a four-wheeler he'd used to drag a board to level his newly terraced backyard into the bed of a pickup. He was nearly up the ramps when the machine raised up and veered back on him, rolling him ass over teakettle. When the horror and the motion stopped, his legs were folded over his head, and the four-wheeler was upside down on top of him, fracturing his L-5 vertebra. I wanted to touch him. To lay my hands on and heal him, use the healing touch therapy I had learned years ago in nursing school, where the transfer of human energy is accomplished by cupping and hovering the hands over the injured body part. I'd seen this in action as a girl, in the Pentecostal churches my family attended. Then I thought that sort of healing was spiritual, or even of the imagi-nation. But I'd witnessed as a nurse what healing touch therapy could do to relax an anxious patient prior to surgery, read the research about im-proved surgical outcomes and faster healing rates for those subjected to it. But my son wanted none of it. I'd left him to learn self-sufficiency, and that's what he relied on. He lay on his back on the floor of the lower level of his home for six weeks. He didn't want my mother love. Only his wife's and his own children's. I, he said, had been too pushy about my voodoo approach to healing.

In my thirties, when I was working as a public health director for the Indian Health Service, lost and alone and without my sons, who I'd sent to live with their fuckhole of a father while I recovered from the trauma of a lost pregnancy, I organized a wellness fair on the reservation. We hired a massage therapist to give people neck rubs. I had to be talked into it. I could let a stranger suckle my tits, but allowing a woman to massage my neck was much more intimate, more personal. I was accustomed to receiving pain; in fact, I sought it out. "Beat me," I used to tell the man I'd picked up. "Knock me around. Hurt me."

But no one ever would. "I'm not that guy," I heard time and again.

She touched me, the woman at the wellness fair, and for a moment, life turned into one big melt. I was on duty in the middle of an Indian reservation in Idaho, far from every member of my family, including my children. Everyone was looking to me to run the day. I couldn't give in to what I felt.

But I did make an appointment.

In those days, what I knew of massage were the sleazy joints in Louisville, across the river from New Albany, Indiana, where I grew up, places where massage was a euphemism for paid coitus. Much later I learned of a phenomenon known as a "happy ending." You could pay a trained hand to jack you off once those same capable hands had softened and weakened the resolve in the rest of your muscles—the bulk of you goes limp in contrast to the part of you that goes hard, leading the way for that final convulsion, rockets, fireworks, all the benefits of the massage therapy undone. I doubt the therapist at the wellness fair traded in happy endings—at least not that kind. Her office was in a modern Spokane building, the walls sage green, not velvet red. The table was padded, heated, the sheets sterile. I could remove my clothes or not.

A friend of mine wrote his master's thesis on the notion of cellular memory. I didn't learn about this until after the massage therapist drizzled my naked back with almond oil. The moment she touched the inferior aspect of the trapezius muscle under my left shoulder blade, the moment she increased the pressure and began to knead, I understood. That's where I had stored it all—the slapped bare ass of my infancy, the bottle propped on the pillow, stuffed into my mouth whether or not I was hungry, the lashings with the patent leather belt and the redbud switch, the screaming mouth of my mother telling me how stupid I was and how quickly and surely my childhood deeds were transporting me to Hell, the fear of the snakes and lizards prowling our sixty-two Indiana acres, the fingers of Mom's stepfather guiding me, guiding me, to prepare to receive him, the anal rape in the boyfriend's van, Ricky, his enormous penis in my rectum right before he shot his wad onto my back. The moment she touched that spot, the sobs began, and I could not stop them. But neither did she stop. She asked if I knew what it was. I told her about my sons, that I had let them—sent them—to go live with their abusive father because the man I was living with, Ricky, insisted on it. That I was ashamed about the pregnancy, sad but glad I'd lost the baby, whose deformities were incompatible with my life.

She told me her story, about her sons who did the same thing, of their own volition, preferring their father's machismo and bravado to her quiet style and peaceful way of living. She too cried. And at the end of the session, she held me in her arms, rocking me side to side, a swaying motion not unlike that of a mother cradling and trying to soothe her baby.

Eggshells

BONNIE BOUCHER

The signs were there when he was an infant. He didn't like to be swaddled, and he would only let certain people snuggle with him. He liked to lay on the arm of the couch, with his arms open and free while he drank his bottle. It hurt his maternal grandmother's feelings because she wanted to interact with him the way she interacted with her other grandchildren when they were babies. His paternal grandmother desperately wanted to embrace him, yet he would pull away from her. In her excitement, she would make a happy screeching sound when she saw him, yet the loudness of her enthusiasm pushed him away. Some people assumed we didn't want to share our son, but that wasn't it. We wanted to protect him. We knew that he was easily overwhelmed and often uncomfortable with what others thought was normal.

We learned that our son has sensory processing disorder, which means that he is often oversensitive to things in his environment, which includes sounds, smells, textures, and touch. But we could also tell that there was more to it than just being oversensitive. When he was in the fourth grade, he was diagnosed with obsessive-compulsive disorder. His OCD is largely affected by his senses—what he sees, hears, and feels. Things have to feel "right" to be okay, which affects everything, and it's a very hard thing to accomplish.

There are also so many rules around touch in our home. Our son doesn't want to be touched on his left side. If you touch his left side, you must touch his right side in the exact same way (as if that's even possible), and the right side must be touched more. The "more" could mean that it's a longer touch, or maybe it's a stronger touch. If you don't touch the right side correctly (to even out having touched the left side), he might even grab your hand to *make* you do it. This feels like a violation—for someone to grab your hand and force you to touch him. I have explained to him, many times, that he cannot do this. He cannot grab someone's hand and force any kind of touch, even if it's to "take away" or "neutralize" the way someone touched him. He doesn't seem to get it. Why can't he grab my hand to "fix" the way I touched him, when I violated him in the first place by touching him in the wrong way? When I think of it this way, it kind of makes sense. He experiences touch differently than most people.

The intrusion of touch extends to his ears when the sound waves touch his eardrums. Sounds can be very disturbing to him—chewing, eating, or any other smacking sounds. And if those sounds are entering his left ear, it's increasingly overwhelming. He also wears a hat whenever he is in the sun. He said the sunlight is "painful" when it touches his head.

He's fourteen now. He's intelligent and quirky. He has a big heart, and he's sentimental. He likes hugs, but only if done correctly. A hug must be firm, and there absolutely cannot be any rubbing. Rubbing ruins everything. A firm squeeze will do, but don't forget that you cannot put more pressure on the left side. No, don't lean your head against him. Just shift your body and lean in, but don't lean in too much. At the same time, you'd better lean in enough. There, that's okay, almost. Wait, no . . . you are touching the left side. Ugh! There are so many rules!

Kisses. Kisses are horrible. They are wet and noisy, and lips touch you when you are kissed. We got away with it when he was a baby, and even a toddler. We could give him kisses on his cheeks, and he didn't complain. But it wasn't long before he rejected any kind of kiss. That was hard—having a young child you couldn't kiss. It literally took years, but I finally found an acceptable replacement. I discovered that he'll let me touch my right cheek to his right cheek. I wish I'd thought of doing that sooner.

The complicated thing is that he actually wants touch, and he needs touch. It just has to be in his way. The rigidity is off-putting, and to many it's strange. When he's having a more difficult day and needs comfort, it also means that he's having a day when he's more sensitive to touch. There are times when I end up standing there, with my arms to my sides, as he hugs me. I have to refrain from hugging him back then, because I'd have to touch him. Thankfully this doesn't happen all of the time. It's not the hug I wish I could have, but it's something. I want him to know that I'm there for him. I'm his mom, and I love him. But I hate OCD, and I hate the rules around touch.

The discomfort is real. When he was younger, his dad and I would step into his room after he was asleep . . . asleep and defenseless . . . so we could give him a kiss on the cheek or a kiss on the forehead without any complaints. But even in his sleep, he pulls away from sounds in his left ear or touch on his left side. Now he's older, and we still slip into his room after he's asleep to check on him. We approach him on his right side, and we might touch our forehead to his forehead to say goodnight. We never dare to kiss him.

I remind myself that it's okay that he's different. Maybe there's even a reason—a reason we can't understand right now. But we worry. What is this going to mean for him as he gets older? I think he'll be able to hold someone's hand, as long as it's his right hand, of course. But the other stuff—kissing, touching, and someday even having sex? I can't even imagine him being able to tolerate the sounds and the touching that would be involved in an intimate relationship. His dad and I hope he'll find someone who has patience and who will love him as he is.

We've learned that one in fifty people has OCD. The label of OCD is given when a person's obsessions and compulsions are intrusive, and they interfere with his/her life. However, it's a vast label. If someone has the diagnosis of OCD, it could mean a variety of things. It could mean that he/she obsesses over moral or religious themes. It could mean that the person worries about contamination. It could mean that the person obsessively worries about doing something that might harm another person, and it could mean that the person obsesses about things feeling "right" or doing things in the "right" way. The intermixing of OCD manifestations can vary for every person, and it can continuously change and evolve for the person who has it.

My husband and I believe that our son has what is referred to as "Just Right" OCD. Our son disagrees, saying it's not "Just Right" OCD. I believe that his opposition to the label actually makes our point, because he doesn't think the label is "right." Regardless of what you call it, the OCD we live with affects everything. It affects how our son gets out of bed in the morning—he scoots down to the foot of the bed before stepping onto the floor. He doesn't ever get out of bed from the side. (I wonder if this will change as he gets older and it becomes physically more difficult to scoot to the end of the bed.) The OCD affects how he brushes his teeth and how he gets dressed. It affects what he eats for breakfast and how he eats it. It affects what type of fork he uses to eat his toast. That's right. He eats toast with a fork. As I mentioned before, there are so many rules involved in making him (or rather making his OCD) comfortable. I know his dad and I are both exhausted. Imagine how the person experiencing OCD must feel. He's constantly on high alert, making sure things are done in the correct way, to help him feel more comfortable. Touch, and the rules around touch, is just one part of a much larger issue.

My husband and I made the decision to be open about our son's OCD and about our struggles. That's how we have found a lot of support. We have learned that if you are open with people, they tend to be open with you.

As our son has gotten older, I've wondered if he'll tell us to stop talking about it, but so far that hasn't happened. Last year in school he had a teacher who confided in us that she, too, struggled with OCD. That teacher ended up being a great advocate for our son as we were trying to get help for him at school. Now, as we just started a new school year, we had a different teacher share that he too has struggled with OCD. Wow! I almost feel guilty that it made me happy to hear that, but the happiness is knowing that he just might understand our situation, and it might help him to have patience. Our son's face lit up when he learned about his teacher. How nice to know that you're not the only one.

The Book

ALISON STONE

Nothing needs to be touched
except bodies.
When the child lies crying
in the mother's arms,
when the father smooths
the satin of her face,
the book of her life
begins to write itself
in a language beautiful and true.

Nothing needs to be touched
except bodies.
When the body of the boy
is cut by his father's belt.
When the body of the girl
is opened,
when the river of the brother's pain
or the sister's pain
flows to the ear of the child,
then disease is scrawled upon the pages
of the body's book.

The man can read the child's story
in the woman's flesh.

His fingers scan boustrophedonic chapters
while his body mimics love.
What is hurt and weak in her calls out
to what is hurt and cruel in him.
They are locked together
like a corpse and its shadow.

Deep beneath the skin
where spirit joins the bones
lies the pool that is the many lifetimes
of the woman or the man.
Injuries and crimes float,
bloated, dank,
while the book
of the true and beautiful is drowned.

The rare woman or man
who is both lucky and brave
will dive into the lake
to shine a candle on the hidden wounds
and speak their truth
until the body lets go
of the story of the parents.
Then the book of life, though worn
and shorter than the child's book,
holds beneath its covers
pages that remain to be written.

touch redux

Regaining Touch with Our Humanity

SUSAN J. TWEIT

When social distancing and shelter in place became "things" in response to the COVID-19 pandemic, I figured I was prepared. As a friend said, "At last, a skill set I can use!" I'm an introvert and a writer: alone time is a necessity for me. And I've been a widow for nearly a decade, so I'm quite used to my own company.

I'm also a natural distancer; I live in a body studded with what feels like thousands of tiny antennae tuned to sensory information. It's easy to be overwhelmed by humanity's din: the tone of our voices, the noise of our digital devices, our volatile emotions, and the electricity of our metabolic energy.

Normally, I dispel that onslaught of nonverbal information by limiting my social contact, spending hours writing and reading, or by solo physical activity: hiking, digging in my garden, or renovating my house. And also—and this may seem counterintuitive, but it is critical—through physical touch with friends and family. Unlike the rest of the sensory stimuli that come my way, that familiar and familial tactile connection is both comforting and soothing.

Research supports the quieting and calming effect of gentle touch on our emotions, our metabolisms, and our overall health—body, mind, and spirit. Touch is a literal balm, and also a bond. When I am frazzled and struggling to keep my emotional and mental balance, the warmth of a friend's hand, a hug, or even the press of a dog's muzzle on my leg helps me settle.

That need for regular touch is part of why I decided last summer it was time to alter my determinedly solo state and open my life to a dog again.

I was driving to Wyoming to teach a seminar at a spiritual retreat center when I asked the universe for a dog, and promised I'd take the next one that came along. The very next day, up wandered a gentlemanly, white-muzzled bird-dog—who came with a guy and The Guy's four horses. Apparently, the universe has quite a sense of humor, because I really did just want a dog . . .

Over the next few months, my life filled with bodily contact: snuggling with the dog, being nuzzled by the horses, and sleeping skin-to-skin with The Guy. It was the bounty of loving company I needed, even if I hadn't known that. Then the COVID-19 crisis brought social distancing and shelter in place. Within a week of my state shutting down, my new herd, two- and four-legged, headed for The Guy's farm, 400 miles away. It was spring, and farm chores couldn't wait: the hayfields needed prepping, irrigation pipes had to be laid out, ditches wanted cleaning, and the tractor and implements needed tuning up.

As the big truck and the horse trailer pulled away, I realized I was alone in a way I had never been, despite living solo for years. With social distancing and no household members in residence, I could no longer touch or be touched. There would be no hugging friends, holding hands with my nieces, getting a massage, or even fist-bumping the guys who fixed my flat tire.

By the time it was safe to rejoin my herd a month later, I was starved for physical contact. I felt ungrounded and unstable, more lonely than I had ever imagined. It's not surprising: humans are, after all, a herd species. No matter how solitary we may think ourselves, we need touch; without it, we become alienated from our own humanness. That alienation is why babies who are not held develop attachment disorders, and prisoners in solitary confinement often succumb to mental illness. Without physical contact, the skin-to-skin bond that tethers us to our own species, and thus to life itself, is severed.

After the prolonged social isolation of COVID-19, perhaps it's no coincidence that we are finally confronting racism and the horrifying brutality that goes with it. What we thought was normal has been entirely upended. Could this be our opportunity to reimagine what is possible and build a society that "matches our scenery," as Wallace Stegner wrote? A society able to offer everyone—regardless of skin color, gender, sexual orientation, religious beliefs—equal justice, education, and equal opportunities to liberty and the pursuit of happiness?

To rise to that ideal, we need to act from the best of our shared humanity. That includes reconnecting through the simple but profound gesture of physical touch—when that's appropriate, and once it's safe to reach for each other again.

Me Tangere/Noli Me Tangere

SARAH KOTCHIAN

When my husband and I were dating in our twenties, he took me to meet his extended family at a summer reunion. As we drove up to the house, the entire family trooped out to line the driveway, twenty or more people interested in meeting his new girlfriend. To me, it felt less like a welcoming committee and more like a gauntlet. Embarrassingly, as I made my way down the line, meeting his parents, siblings, and cousins, my body began to shake, my lips to quiver. I was beginning to fall apart from the nerves of passing inspection—and I did so want to pass muster. Aunt Peggy was about two-thirds of the way down the row. Whether she was just being herself or saw my predicament and took action, she stepped forward out of line, gave me a big bear hug, and announced, "Any friend of Bobby's is a friend of mine!"

That strong long-lasting hug, her symbolic, kind embrace of my vulnerability in that moment, restored me to myself. I stopped shaking and was able to laugh; the ice was broken. At ninety-seven she is still an example of how you can make someone feel welcome through touch—in this case, the accepting hug of a new family. It's entirely possible that hugging has contributed to her longevity.

The word "tangible," meaning capable of being touched, comes from the Latin "tangere," to touch. What is it about touch, physical contact, that seems superficial yet causes a tactile storm that literally runs deep throughout our bodies? We are equipped with internal wiring, thousands of receptors that activate our nervous system, sending signals to our brain about what part of our body is being touched and whether that touch is pleasurable or painful. We feel touch on our skin, which also marks the threshold of all that is not-me, the tangible and intangible outer world. The sensation on this outer surface of our bodies—pressure, texture, temperature—gives us the impression that we and other objects in our world are impermeable. Yet we are in fact physically permeable—a collection of atoms and molecules encased by millimeters of skin that is itself permeable. As I learned from Aunt Peggy, touch can restore our ground of being, our sense of wholeness when we become uncentered. We are porous in the emotional sense, able to merge with the energy, bodies, spirits of another in moments of tenderness and intimacy, but also vulnerable to unwelcome contact.

"Good" touch in appropriate amounts at the right time lets us know we are valued, worthwhile, cherished. Research shows that cuddling and close pleasurable contact causes our bodies to release the hormone oxytocin, nicknamed "the bonding hormone," which gives us a sense of well-being. Babies who receive regular soothing touch begin early to build a sense of self-worth, while babies deprived of touch, such as those in overcrowded orphanages, fail to thrive. In recognition of this, more and more hospitals immediately place the newborn in skin-to-skin contact with the mother for increased bonding in the first minutes and hours of life.

I have many pleasant early memories of touch with my grandmother. While she read to us, we snuggled next to her on the couch, burrowing into her cushioned body in a flowered dress. We live in a society obsessed with hard bodies, yet there is such great comfort in plump bodies that accommodate us in their amplitude. At night she read us a bedtime story, and as my sister and I lay in our twin beds, she would flutter her fingers down upon our eyelids, sprinkling sleepy dust on them. I can still feel her smooth, cool fingers, and hear her soft voice as she whispered down the sleepy dust, a magical send-off into dreamland.

Because touch is necessary for life and well-being, the emotional impact of our required separation during the recent COVID pandemic has been devastating and far-reaching. "Wash your hands!" "Keep your distance from others!" We are told not to touch even our own faces. Grandparents have not been able to touch their grandchildren. Our visits to the elderly in nursing homes, our bedside visits to the sick and dying, our street ministries to the homeless and others we used to touch have been sharply curtailed. Children are not able to play with friends, to run around together at recess, to socialize over lunch in the cafeteria. Teachers who already refrained from hugging now cannot touch the students at all out of fear of spreading COVID. This enforced separation affects the mental health of our communities, ourselves included. Depression and despair are on the rise, accompanied by increases in suicide and domestic violence. Our physical isolation affects both the toucher and the touched.

The pandemic has been particularly hard on those who grieve. The physical loss of a loved one is one reason that grief itself is also physical, deeply personal, beyond words. It is as if our insides have been hollowed out, our neural pathways short-circuited. We feel the absence of touch keenly. When we lose the sense of the tangible, it seems we lose our very sense of self. When we could gather around a loved one, hug, sit side by side, spend as much time as possible in enclosed spaces talking softly and leaning closely together, our tangibility and warmth provided some comfort in the loss. Now, however, when people cannot grieve together, cannot hold funerals in the presence of friends and families, the isolation is even more pronounced.

The words "noli me tangere" come to me, and I am reminded of a scriptural passage in which the risen Christ appears in the garden to Mary, one of his followers. "Noli me tangere," he says, "Do not touch me." Some scholars believe he was telling Mary that from then on, theirs would be a bond of the spirit. He would be present, but not in the same physical way. He was encouraging her to have faith in the enduring love of their remembered relationship. During COVID time, we also have had to rely on that trust, our memories of time once spent together, to keep us whole until we can meet again.

I remember the last hug I gave and received, as I expect most of us do during this time of COVID. I was with an older friend who is starting to be forgetful. We had been visiting on the porch at the proper social distance, and when she and her husband stood up to leave, she forgot and hugged us goodbye while he stood helplessly some feet away, shaking his head and saying apologetically, "Breaking all the rules." During this time especially, there are so many new rules, spoken and unspoken, and yet our natural urge is to override them and hug one another.

It is so important to reach out and be "in touch" with loved ones, and at the same time, it is not actual touch. Unable to travel freely and to gather, we gaze at our photos and videos of loved ones, lean into our touch screens to bring up a Zoom view, have an electronic "FaceTime." We are all hungry for contact. I have dreams in which my phone touch screen isn't working, where the home button doesn't respond, where I can't pull up my contacts and find an address, where the telephone function isn't working. My dreams remind me that I am seeking real touch, not a touch screen, a slow conversation instead of Zoom, real face-to-face time instead of "FaceTime." I am grateful for the technologies that allow us to see the faces of our loved ones and colleagues, but I know that they are not substitutes for the real thing.

Nevertheless, as wonderful as are the benefits, there are other, darker aspects of touch. The decision to touch or not to touch goes to the heart of true intimacy and vulnerability, culture, and power. Touch can harm us or save us. All of us have, at some time in our lifetime, experienced touch of both kinds, and our stories carry both our shame and our delight. Because of our deep need for touch and our desire to be vulnerable with another, our bodies are sacred. We want and deserve to be subjects, not objects. When we are babies and children, we depend on other trusted adults to care for us, to minister to our bodies with appropriate loving touch, changing, bathing, feeding, holding, cuddling. As we become aware of our own separate personhood, it is important to us to have our boundaries respected, to be taught and encouraged to assert our agency and right to privacy, to indicate whether or not we give consent to having our personal space entered by another.

Yet so often those personal margins are not respected, particularly for women and those with less power in a culture. Touch that is unwanted, harsh, insensitive, or violent invades our boundaries and our privacy. Inappropriate touch violates our personhood, causing emotional and psychological wounds that may never fully heal. When those with power over others abuse that power, the inequity in the situation undermines the recipient's ability to give meaningful consent or to refuse touch.

All is not well in our world, particularly in our nation at this time. As evidenced by the Black Lives Matter protests, we are learning that our country has never been truly well, with a sickness and a shame at its heart that cannot be cured until exposed to the light and touch of truth, acknowledgment, lament, painful healing, and love. While visiting our son and his wife who had newly relocated to Alabama, I happened to come across the history of the Alabama flag. The current flag features a red cross on a white background. However, for the Alabama Secession Convention in 1861, the ladies of Montgomery sewed a special flag that flew over the capitol for one month. On one side it featured the Goddess of Liberty with a sword upheld in one hand. On the other side, it had a rattlesnake coiled at the base of a cotton plant, with the words "Noli me tangere." I felt a chill as I read this; the flag makers had taken a scriptural passage acknowledging the need for faith in spiritual bonds and converted its meaning to a violent one. The message in 1861 was clear: "If you mess with me and my traditions, my cotton-growing practices and the slavery it requires, I will smite you with a raised sword and a sudden strike of deadly venom." "Don't touch me" meant "Don't interfere with the way we do things here." Even more, it meant that we are only a union when we all agree to let each person and state do as they please regardless of human rights and ethics—American individualism taken to its extreme. We hear that same separatist rhetoric today: my rights outweigh my responsibility for yours—requiring me to wear a mask, for instance, interferes with my individual liberty.

Touch is one of the key entry points for developing empathy and compassion as well as for healing. Many faith traditions use a "laying on of hands" to confer blessing, healing, ordination, spiritual power. Our nationwide conversation over the past year has begun to create an awareness about the barriers we have created between us on many levels. We acknowledge that the very obstacles we have knowingly and unknowingly designed are preventing us from reaching our full capacity for compassion. My recent reencounter with the phrase "noli me tangere" caused me to ponder further the concept of touch as an exclusionary boundary in our world as well as one that embraces. Who are we not touching when we say, "Don't touch me?" Who are the untouchables in our society? When we refuse to see or to touch, we withhold blessing and healing, and because touch works in both directions, we receive none in return. Isolated within homogenous units, we cannot be blessed and healed by relationships with the poor, the homeless, the addicted, with those who look different, the incarcerated, the elderly, the shut-ins, those who are not only untouchable but often invisible to us. If we know the value of appropriate touch, what must we also acknowledge about the consequences of not touching or being touched? Our separation has kept our nation in a self-absorbed emotional adolescence. Perhaps this time of reckoning will allow our country to grow into a mature, interdependent adulthood.

I know that when it becomes safe for us to hug again and we step into that tight circle without the six-foot distance, I may not be able to let go for a long time. I may very well weep at the pure joy and the physical pleasure of its love and intimacy. As our nervous systems come alive at touch,

I hope that our compassion and empathy will come alive as well. I hope that our consciousness remains awakened about who is in the circle and who needs to be welcomed in, about who might be an untouchable who desperately needs touch, along with an awareness about how we, too, suffer when others are estranged from us. I dream that the lessons we have learned and the strategies we have used to maintain community during COVID will prompt us to move forward, not back to our old, isolated ways. We might even begin to think of ourselves as a new family. I hope the practice of "don't touch me, and I won't touch you" will evolve into "let's create a new world, shoulder to shoulder." It is not a matter of charity. It is essential to our survival, this coming to understand our interdependent kinship with all of life. And, like my Aunt Peggy, we all may live longer because of it.

Miriam, Quarantined

ERIKA DREIFUS

> So Miriam was shut out of camp seven days; and the
> people did not march on until Miriam was readmitted.
>
> —Numbers 12:15

Had another been stricken on the way to the promised land—
had the Divine perhaps punished my brother Aaron
(who, may the record show, was equally at fault)—
I'd have cared for the patient,
no matter how feverish, or contagious, or leprous.

But when *I* was the one afflicted and the Divine refused
my other brother's plea for mercy,
none sat by my side, or brought me water,
or smoothed my brow.

Cast out to suffer seven days in solitude
I knew not what would greet me
once the snow-white scales had faded,
the skin refreshed,
the illness and banishment ended.

How miraculous the discovery:
The people had remained.
How indescribable
the emotions as we set out anew,
together.

Contributors

Joan Schweighardt has worked as an editor and ghostwriter for private and corporate clients for more than twenty-five years. She had her own independent publishing company, GreyCore Press, from 1999 to 2005. Several of her titles have won awards, including a Barnes & Noble "Discover Great New Writers," a *ForeWord Magazine* "Best Fiction of the Year," and a Borders "Top Ten Read to Me." She has agented books as well, with sales to St. Martin's, Red Hen, Wesleyan University Press, and more. Schweighardt's most recent fiction is the Rivers Trilogy—*Before We Died* (2018), *Gifts for the Dead* (2019), and *River Aria* (2020). She has written additional novels, a memoir, children's books, and magazine articles. Website: www.joanschweighardt.com.

Faye Rapoport DesPres is the author of the memoir in essays *Message from a Blue Jay* (2014), the *Stray Cat Stories* (2018–21) children's book series, and *Soul to Soul: Tiny Stories of Hope and Resilience* (2023). Her work has appeared in a variety of literary journals, including *Ascent, Bending Genres, Connotation Press: An Online Artifact* (where four of her contributions were selected for "best of the year" annual issues), and *Superstition Review.* Her journalism has appeared in *The New York Times, Trail and Timberline*, and other publications. A graduate of Brandeis University, the SUNY College of Environmental Science and Forestry, and the Solstice MFA in Creative Writing program, she has taught writing at Lasell University and in programs for adults and children. Website: www.faye rapoportdespres.com.

María Luisa Arroyo Cruzado, born in Manatí, Puerto Rico, and raised in Springfield, Massachusetts, earned her undergraduate and graduate degrees in German, her third language. She also earned an MFA in creative writing (poetry) from the Solstice MFA Program. Part of María Luisa's lifelong learning as a multilingual Boricua poet and intersectional feminist educator is to reclaim her Puerto Rican español by excavating living and buried family stories and oral histories on the island and in the diaspora. Her published collections include *Gathering Words: Recogiendo palabras* (2008) and two chapbooks, *Flight* (2016) and *Destierro Means More Than Exile* (2018).

Donna Baier Stein is the author of *The Silver Baron's Wife* (2016, PEN/New England Discovery Award, Foreword Reviews Winner, and other awards), *Sympathetic People* (2013, Iowa Fiction Award finalist), *Letting Rain Have Its Say* (2018), and *Scenes from the Heartland* (2019, Foreword Reviews finalist). A founding editor of *Bellevue Literary Review*, she founded and publishes *Tiferet Journal*. She has received a Bread Loaf Scholarship, Johns Hopkins University Fellowship, and other awards. Donna's writing appears in *Virginia Quarterly Review, Washingtonian, Next Avenue, Saturday Evening Post, Writer's Digest*, and many other literary journals, as well as in *I've Always Meant to Tell You* (Pocket Books) and *To Fathers: What I've Never Said* (featured in *O Magazine*). She teaches writing classes through *Tiferet Journal* and The Writers Circle.

Magdalena Ball was born in New York City, where she grew up. After gaining an honours degree in English Literature from the City University of New York, she moved to Oxford in the United Kingdom to study English literature at a postgraduate level. She then migrated to NSW Australia, where she now resides on a rural property with her family. Magdalena is a novelist, poet, reviewer, and interviewer, and is the managing editor of *Compulsive Reader*, a well-respected book review site now in its twenty-fourth year. She is the author of a number of novels and poetry books, the most recent of which, *The Density of Compact Bone*, was published in 2021 by Ginninderra Press. She has won or been shortlisted in a number of Australian and international competitions. Find out more about Magdalena at http://www.magdalenaball.com.

Bonnie Boucher is a parent who also happens to be a clinical mental health counselor. Although she is a licensed therapist, her education and training didn't prepare her for raising a son who suffers from OCD. Bonnie's background has helped her be an advocate for her son and to want to learn more about the diagnosis and how to help others who struggle with the multifaceted, fascinating, and overwhelming symptoms associated with OCD. To refresh and reboot from life stressors, Bonnie enjoys talking with friends and expressing herself creatively through a variety of activities, such as painting, making jewelry, decoupage, sculpting with polymer clay, writing rhymes, and baking for her family.

Anne Casey is an Irish poet/writer living in Australia, and author of four poetry collections. A journalist, magazine editor, legal author, and media communications director for thirty years, her work ranks in the leading national daily newspaper, *The Irish Times*', Most Read list, and is widely published and anthologized internationally. Anne has won literary prizes in Ireland, the United Kingdom, the United States, Canada, Hong Kong, and Australia—most recently the *American Writers Review 2021* and the *2021 iWoman Global Award* for *Literature*. She is the recipient of an Australian government scholarship for her PhD in creative writing at the University of Technology Sydney. anne-casey.com @1annecasey.

Joy Castro is the award-winning author of the novels *One Brilliant Flame* (2023) and *Flight Risk* (2021), the post-Katrina New Orleans literary thrillers *Hell or High Water* (2012) and *Nearer Home* (2013), and the story collection *How Winter Began* (2015), as well as the memoir *The Truth Book* (2012) and the essay collection *Island of Bones* (2012), which received the International Latino Book Award. She is also editor of the anthology *Family Trouble* (2013) and served as the guest judge of CRAFT's first Creative Nonfiction Award. Her work has appeared in *The New York Times Magazine*, *Senses of Cinema*, *Salon*, *Ploughshares*, *Gulf Coast*, *Brevity*, *Afro-Hispanic Review*, and elsewhere. A former writer in residence at Vanderbilt University, she is currently the Willa Cather Professor of English and Ethnic Studies at the University of Nebraska–Lincoln.

Quintin Collins (he/him) is a writer, editor, and Solstice MFA Program assistant director. He is the author of *The Dandelion Speaks of Survival* (Cherry Castle Publishing, 2021) and *Claim Tickets for Stolen People* (The Ohio State University Press/Mad Creek Books, 2022), and was selected by Marcus Jackson as winner of *The Journal's* 2020 Charles B. Wheeler Prize. Quintin's other awards and accolades include a Pushcart Prize and the 2019 Atlantis Award from the Poet's Billow, as well as Best of the Net nominations.

Paula Coomer is a poet and literary fiction writer who occasionally writes about food and health. Her writing has appeared in many journals, anthologies, and online publications. Her books include the novels *Jagged Edge of the Sky* (2016) and *Dove Creek* (2006), the short story collections *Somebody Should Have Scolded the Girl* (2019) and *Summer of Government Cheese* (2007, 2011), and the poetry collections *Nurses Who Love English* (2013) and *Devil at the Crossroads* (2006). A food memoir, *Blue Moon Vegetarian* (2015, 2016), was followed by the much-loved cookbook *Blue Moon Vegan*. A long-time teacher of writing, Ms. Coomer has been a nominee for the Pulitzer, the Pushcart, and others. She lives with her husband, Phil, in the tiny town of Garfield, Washington, where she coaches writers and organizes and facilitates Clearwater Writers, a retreat program on the wild and scenic Clearwater River near Syringa, Idaho.

Laura Crucianelli is a Marie Skłodowska-Curie Research Fellow at the Brain, Body and Self Lab in the Department of Neuroscience at the Karolinska Institute in Stockholm, and an honorary research associate at the Research

Department of Clinical, Educational, and Health Psychology at University College London.

Linda DeFruscio-Robinson, in addition to her work as an electrologist, is the author of the memoir *Cornered: Dr. Richard J. Sharp, As I Knew Him* (2015), the collection *Transgender Profiles: Time for a Change* (2018), and the children's books *Ginger and Moe and the Incredible Coincidence* (2016) and *Love Tails from the Wall* (2020, coauthored with her husband, Greg Robinson).

Erika Dreifus is the author of *Birthright: Poems* (2019, Kelsay Books) and *Quiet Americans: Stories* (2011, Last Light Studio), which was named a Sophie Brody Medal honor title for outstanding achievement in Jewish literature. A fellow in the Sami Rohr Literary Institute, she teaches at Baruch College of The City University of New York. Since 2004, Erika has published *The Practicing Writer*, a free (and popular) e-newsletter for writers of fiction, poetry, and creative nonfiction. Visit her online at ErikaDreifus.com and follow her on Twitter @Erika Dreifus, where she tweets "on matters bookish and/or Jewish."

Rafael Frumkin is a nonbinary trans man and author of *The Comedown* (Henry Holt, 2018). His fiction, nonfiction, journalism, and criticism have been featured in *The Paris Review*, *Washington Post*, *Granta*, *McSweeney's*, *The Baffler*, *Poetry Magazine*, *Outside*, *Pacific Standard*, *Best American Nonrequired Reading*, and *Guernica*. He is an assistant professor of creative writing at Southern Illinois University, where he's by far the gayest person in the department. His second novel, *Confidence*, is about two con men, sometimes lovers, who pull off a massive global scheme on the scale of Theranos. His third book is a collection of short stories about things such as BDSM porn families and mania and Kimye. The latter two books are forthcoming from Simon and Schuster in 2023 and 2024, respectively. Find him online at @jeansvaljeans.

Nicole Hardy is the author of the 2013 memoir *Confessions of a Latter-Day Virgin* (Hyperion). She's best known for her *Modern Love* essay "Single Female Mormon Alone," which is featured on the *Modern Love* podcast and noted in 2012's *Best American Essays*. She earned her MFA at the Bennington College Writing Seminars.

Will Jennings's poetry, essays, and creative nonfiction have appeared in *The Water~Stone Review*, *Fourth Genre*, *The Southern Humanities Review*, *River Teeth*, *Fugue*, and *The Wapsipinicon Almanac* and have been anthologized by both the University of Chicago and Ice Cube Presses. His work was awarded the Brenda Ueland Prose Prize, has received numerous Pushcart nominations, and has been recognized as an essay of note. His sequenced-essay-memoir *How I Know*

Orion is to be published by Ice Cube Press in 2023. He lives in Iowa City, Iowa, and Woolwich, Maine, with his wife, author Susan Futrell. He still aspires to play center field for the Chicago White Sox.

Meg Kearney's latest poetry collection is *All Morning the Crows*, winner of the 2020 Washington Prize, and spent seven months on SPD's poetry bestseller list after its release in 2021. Other collections include *An Unkindness of Ravens* (BOA Editions, 2001) and *Home by Now* (Four Way Books, 2009), winner of the 2010 PEN New England LL Winship Award and a finalist for *Forward Magazine's* book of the year. Meg is also author of three critically acclaimed novels-in-verse for teens. Her award-winning picture book *Trouper* (Scholastic, 2013) features illustrations by E. B. Lewis. Meg has taught poetry at The New School University and is founding director of the Solstice MFA in Creative Writing Program at Lasell University. Her poetry has been featured on Poetry Daily, Ted Kooser's "American Life in Poetry" series, and Garrison Keillor's "A Writer's Almanac." A native New Yorker, Meg now lives in New Hampshire. For more information, visit www.megkearney.com.

Becky Kennedy is a linguist and a professor; she lives with her family in Jamaica Plain, Massachusetts. She earned her AB in English at Radcliffe College, and her PhD in linguistics at Harvard University; her publications in theoretical and applied linguistics include articles and a book. Her poetry has appeared in magazines and journals and in two chapbooks; her work has been nominated for the Pushcart Prize and has appeared on *Verse Daily*.

Sarah Kotchian's *Camino* (2014), a book of poems about her five-hundred-mile solo pilgrimage in Spain, received the New Mexico and Arizona Book Award and Seven Sisters Book Award. She was a contributor at the 2019 Bread Loaf Writer's Conference, and her work has appeared in *Stoneboat Literary Journal*, *High Shelf Press*, *Tiny Seed Literary Journal*, *Tulip Tree Press*, *Wingless Dreamer*, *Persimmon Tree*, *Bosque Journal*, and *ABQ inPrint*, and on *The Unruly Muse* podcast. Her poetry collection *Light of Wings* is forthcoming from the University of New Mexico Press in 2024. She holds a PhD in American studies from the University of New Mexico, master's degrees in education and public health from Harvard University and the University of Washington, and a BA in American Literature from Middlebury College. She lives at the foot of the Sandia Mountains in New Mexico.

Rocco Lo Bosco is the author of two novels, *Buddha Wept* (Grey Core Press, 2003) and *Ninety-Nine* (Letters At 3 am Press, 2015), and the nonfiction *Staying Sane in Crazy Town: A Monologue of Rude Wisdom* (Waldorf Press, 2019). Additionally, he has coauthored two books with author/psychoanalyst Danielle Knafo: *The Age* *of Perversion: Desire and Technology in Psychoanalysis and Culture* (Routledge Press, 2017) and *The New Sexual Landscape and Contemporary Psychoanalysis* (Confer Books, 2020).

Sarah McElwain, for ten years, taught yoga to the blind at the Lighthouse Guild in New York City. A stress management trainer and restorative yoga teacher, she edits the Integral Yoga Institute of New York newsletter. From 2010 to 2018 she was a cohost of Writers Read NYC, providing reading venues for writers in Greenwich Village. A longtime member of Pulitzer Prize winner Philip Schultz's Writers Studio, she teaches one-on-one tutorials to adults and teenagers. Her recent work has won a Pen American Women Writers SMK award, and has been published in *The Writers Studio at 30*, *Fiction Now*, *SKidROw PeNtHouSe*, and *Epiphany*, as well as recorded as a podcast for *Second Hand Stories* and the *Poets Pandemic Podcast* #8. She is also the editor of *Saying Grace* (Chronicle Books, 2003).

Damian McNicholl was born and educated in Northern Ireland and is a former attorney. His critically acclaimed first novel, *A Son Called Gabriel* (2004, 2017), was an American Booksellers Association *Book Sense Pick* and a finalist in the *Lambda Literary Awards* and *ForeWord Magazine Book of the Year Awards*. His latest novel, *The Moment of Truth* (2017), is published by Pegasus Books. Damian has appeared on CBS, WYBE Public Television, National Public Radio, and other media outlets in the United States and in the United Kingdom to discuss his work. He lives in Bucks County, Pennsylvania. https://www.damianmcnicholl.com.

Lynda Miller grew up in the 1940s and 1950s as a cowgirl in Colorado, where some of her best friends were horses and she could ride for days without seeing another person. Storytelling, often centered around experiences involving horse pals, was paramount in Lynda's Irish family, suffusing her with a love of language. Throughout her life Lynda wrote stories of her own, and as a professional she studied how children learn language and storytelling. Lynda's memoir, *More Horses Than Cars*, was published by Bosque Press in 2021. Currently she's in the finishing stages of a novel about a gay undercover cop in Denver in the mid-1950s, called *Denver Undercover*. Lynda now lives in New Mexico, where she is a writer, artist, and copublisher with Lynn C. Miller of *ABQ inPrint*, an occasional publication that combines art and the written word. She remains enchanted by the magic of language and of horses.

Lynn C. Miller's fourth novel, *The Unmasking*, came out with UNM Press in the fall of 2020. Her third novel, *The Day after Death*, was named a 2017 Lambda Literary Award finalist. Prior published novels are *The Fool's Journey* (2002) and *Death of a Department Chair* (2006). Her short plays and stories have appeared in various periodicals, including *Chautauqua Journal*, where the short story "Words Shimmer" received an editors' prize. She has performed and directed the work of women writers such as Gertrude Stein, Edith Wharton, Victoria Woodhull, and Katherine Anne Porter. Miller taught performance studies and writing at the University of Southern California, Pennsylvania State University, and the University of Texas at Austin, where she was professor of theater and dance until 2007. She is copublisher of Bosque Press, cohost of the podcast *The Unruly Muse*, and lives in Albuquerque, New Mexico. For more information, go to www.lynncmiller.com.

Sarah Moon is a playwright and Assistant Professor of Humanities at Massachusetts Maritime Academy. Her poetry and essays have been published in *Rosebud, The Rambling, H-Net Nutrition*, and *Voices of the Earth: Future of Our Planet II*. Her most recent plays, *Not So Quiet* and *Shrewed Up*, were both produced as audio plays during the pandemic. She is founder and facilitator of the food-centered community writing and performance project Write Your Roots. She lives in Coventry, Connecticut, with her husband and children.

Kate Niles holds an MFA in fiction from Vermont College and is the author of two novels and a book of poetry. She won *ForeWord Magazine*'s Best Fiction Award for Independent Presses for her novel *The Basket Maker* (2004) and has received a Colorado Council of the Arts Individual Fellowship award. She has been published widely and is a Pushcart Prize nominee. She lived in Colorado and the Southwest much of her life but currently lives in Providence, Rhode Island, with her husband and aged cat. Her day job is as a trauma-focused therapist in private practice.

Anne-Marie Oomen's forthcoming books are AWP's winner of the Sue William Silverman nonfiction prize for *As Long as I Know You* (2022, University of Georgia Press), and *The Long Road* (2023, Cornerstone Press). She edited *ELEMENTAL: A Collection of Michigan Nonfiction* (2019) and is the author of *The Lake Michigan Mermaid* (2019, coauthored with Linda Nemec Foster), *Pulling Down the Barn* (2004), *House of Fields* (2008), all Michigan Notable Books, *American Map: Essays* (2010), *Uncoded Woman* (2008, poetry), and *Love, Sex and 4-H* (2015, Next Generation Indie Award for Memoir). She has written seven plays, including the award-winning *Secrets of Luuce Talk Tavern*. She is a poetry and nonfiction instructor at Solstice MFA at Lasell University (Massachusetts) and Interlochen College of Creative Arts. Visit her at www.anne-marieoomen.com.

Alicia Ostriker is a poet and critic. Author of seventeen collections of poetry, she has been twice nominated for the National Book Award and has twice received the National Jewish Book Award for Poetry, among other honors. As a critic she is the author of the now-classic *Stealing the Language: The Emergence* *of Women's Poetry in America* (1986), and other books on poetry and on the Bible, most recently *For the Love of God: The Bible as an Open Book* (2007). Her most recent collections of poems are *Waiting for the Light* (2017) and *The Volcano and After: Selected and New Poems, 2002–2019.* Her poems have been translated into numerous languages, including Hebrew and Arabic. She was recently the New York State Poet Laureate and a chancellor of the Academy of American Poets.

Dr. Christine Page, known as a mystical physician, has been a pioneer in the field of holistic healthcare for over forty years, qualifying as a doctor and homeopath from the University of London. Raised among healers, mediums, and esoteric teachers, she's an international speaker on subjects including enhancing intuition, earth mysteries, soul-centered health, and women's empowerment. A natural intuitive and wise woman, she enjoys teaching others to listen to the messages from the body and the natural world, seeing herself as a communicator that bridges different worlds. She is the author of nine books, including her bestseller *Frontiers of Health* (1992, 2005) and her latest, *The Heart of the Great Mother* (2020). www.christinepage.com.

Robert Root is an emeritus professor of English at Central Michigan University. With Michael Steinberg, he coedited six editions of the anthology *The Fourth Genre: Contemporary Writers of/on Creative Nonfiction* and served as interview/roundtable editor for the journal *Fourth Genre.* He is also the editor of the anthology *Landscapes with Figures: The Nonfiction of Place.* He is the author of the craft text *The Nonfictionist's Guide: On Reading and Writing Creative Nonfiction* (2008), the essay collections *Limited Sight Distance: Essays for Airwaves* (2013) and *Postscripts: Retrospections on Time and Place* (2012), the memoirs *Happenstance* (2013) and *Lineage* (2020), and four literary travel memoirs. He lives in Wisconsin. His website is www.rootwriting.com.

Judith Simon Prager is a writer, therapist, lecturer, and award-winning instructor with her husband, the poet Harry Youtt, in the UCLA Ext Writers' Program. She trains physicians, nurses, first responders, and counselors in the protocol she codeveloped called Verbal First Aid™, lecturing across the United States and around the world, including China, Sweden, Brunei, Northern Ireland, and England. Her books include *The Worst Is Over: What to Say When Every Moment Counts* (2002, 2014) and *Verbal First Aid: Help Your Kids Heal from Fear and Pain and Come Out Strong* (2010, both coauthored with Judith Acosta, LISW), plus her children's book *Owie Cadabra's Verbal First Aid for Kids* (2010), and her latest book, *What the Dolphin Said* (2017). She has a PhD in psychology, has designed one of the first guided imagery programs for before, during, and after surgery for Cedars-Sinai Medical Center, and lives in Los Angeles. https://judithprager.com.

Paul Singer, by day, is an investigative reporter and editor for GBH News in Boston. By night he plays with typewriters. He has done some version of these two things for many years.

Phyllis M Skoy is the author of *What Survives*, a novel set in Turkey (IP Books, 2016), shortlisted for the Santa Fe Writers Project, finalist in the New Mexico/Arizona Book Awards, and first runner-up in the Eric Hoffer Grand Prize short list. *What Survives* was rereleased in April 2022 by Black Rose Writing, along with a second novel in A Turkish Trilogy, *As They Are*, released in June 2022. Skoy is currently working on the third book for the series, *A Coup*. Skoy has also published a family memoir, *Myopia* (IP Books, 2017). Skoy is the author of various short stories and essays. She is a retired psychanalyst and currently resides in Placitas, New Mexico.

Grace Anne Stevens spent over forty years in the tech world, and returned to school at the age of fifty-eight and received her master's in counseling at age sixty-two in 2009. In 2011 she successfully transitioned gender at the age of sixty-four, and in two vastly different workplaces, the technical and counseling worlds. Grace's books include *Handbooks for Humans* (2018), *No! Maybe? Yes! Living My Truth* (2015), and *Musings on Living Authentically* (2016). In July 2016 she was selected as an Amtrak Residency Writer, and in March 2017, Grace was honored to be named "The Person of the Year" by New England Pride TV. Grace is a speaker on gender, diversity, and living authentically. Her website is www.liveurtruth.net.

Alison Stone has published seven full-length collections, *Zombies at the Disco* (Jacar Press, 2020), *Caught in the Myth* (NYQ Books, 2019), *Dazzle* (Jacar Press, 2017), *Masterplan*, a book of collaborative poems with Eric Greinke (Presa Press, 2018), Ordinary Magic (NYQ Books, 2016), *Dangerous Enough* (Presa Press, 2014), and *They Sing at Midnight* (2003), which won the 2003 Many Mountains Moving Poetry Award, as well as three chapbooks. Her poems have appeared in *The Paris Review, Poetry, Ploughshares, Barrow Street, Poet Lore*, and many other journals and anthologies. She has been awarded *Poetry*'s Frederick Bock Prize and *New York Quarterly*'s Madeline Sadin Award. She was writer in Residence at LitSpace St. Petersburg. She is also a painter and the creator of The Stone Tarot. A licensed psychotherapist, she has private practices in NYC and Nyack. www.stonepoetry.org www.stonetarot.com. YouTube—Alison Stone Poetry.

Daniel B. Summerhill is assistant professor of poetry/social action and composition studies at California State University–Monterey Bay. He has performed in over thirty states, and in the United Kingdom, and was invited by the U.S. Embassy to guest lecture and perform in South Africa. Daniel has earned a Sharon Olds fellowship as well as a fellowship from the Watering

Hole. His poetry has appeared in *Columbia Journal*, *Rust & Moth*, *Button Poetry*, *Anti-Heroin Chic*, *The Hellebore*, and others. His work has earned him two Pushcart nominations as well as a Best of the Net nomination. His debut collection is *Divine, Divine, Divine* (2021) published by Oakland-based Nomadic Press. His sophomore collection, *Mausoleum of Flowers*, was published by CavanKerry Press in April 2022. Summerhill holds an MFA in Creative Writing from the Solstice Low-Residency MFA program of Lasell college (Boston). Daniel is the inaugural poet Laureate of Monterey County. www.daniel summerhill.com.

Deborah Swift is an English writer of historical fiction. Before publishing her first novel Deborah worked as a set and costume designer for theatre and BBC TV. She developed a degree course in theatre arts at City College Manchester, where she taught scenography and the history of design. With fourteen novels to date, Deborah's most recent books include *The Occupation* (2019) and *The Lifeline* (2021), and she is currently working on a seventeenth-century trilogy set in Italy. Deborah is a keen blogger about the writing life. www.deborahswift.com.

Beatriz Terrazas is a writer, photographer, and video producer who believes in the transformative power of story. In 1994 she was part of a *Dallas Morning News* team that won the Pulitzer Prize for a global project about violence against women. She's a Nieman Fellow, class of 1999, as well as a member of the American Society of Media Photographers, and the Macondo Writers Workshop. Her magazine credits include *More, D Magazine, The Texas Observer, Texas Highways, 76092 Magazine*, and several anthologies, including *Wise Latinas, Writers on Higher Education* (Jennifer De Leon, University of Nebraska Press), *Literary El Paso* (Marcia Hatfield Daudistel, TCU Press), and *Viva Texas Rivers!* (Steven L. Davis and Sam L. Pfiester, The Wittliff collections Literary Series in partnership with the Meadows Center for Water and the Environment, Texas State University and Texas A&M University Press).

Meg Tuite is author of the novel-in-stories *Domestic Apparition* (San Francisco Bay Press, 2011), the short story collection *Bound by Blue* (Sententia Books, 2013), *Meet My Haze* (Big Table Publishing, 2018), and *White Van* (Unlikely Books, 2022); won the Twin Antlers Collaborative Poetry award (from Artistically Declined Press) for her poetry collection *Bare Bulbs Swinging* (2014); and has written five chapbooks of short fiction, flash, poetic prose, and multigenre work. She teaches workshops and online classes through Bending Genres and is an associate editor at *Narrative Magazine*. Her work has been published in over six hundred literary magazines and over fifteen anthologies, including *Choose Wisely: 35 Women Up to No Good*. She has been nominated over fifteen times for the Pushcart Prize, won first and second place in Prick of the Spindle contest, is a five-time finalist at *Glimmer Train*, a finalist of the Gertrude Stein Award, and won third prize in the Bristol Short Story Contest. She is also the editor of eight anthologies. She is included in *Best Small Fictions* of 2021. Her blog is http://megtuite.com.

Susan J. Tweit, an award-winning writer and plant ecologist, began her career in Wyoming studying grizzly bear habitat—which involved collecting and dissecting bear poop—mapping historic wildfires, and researching big sagebrush. Tweit began writing after realizing that she loved writing the stories behind the data as much as collecting the data. She's written thirteen books, ranging from memoir and nature writing to kid lit and travel, along with hundreds of magazine articles, columns, and essays. Her latest book, *Bless the Birds: Living with Love in a Time of Dying* (2021), has been called "powerful and poignant" and "a rare gift." Tweit's passion is restorying this earth, and we who share the planet, with the hope of leaving this world in better shape than she found it. She lives in a small cottage shaded by tall cottonwood trees in the sagebrush country of western Colorado. Read her work at susanjtweit.com.

Printed in the USA
CPSIA information can be obtained
at www.ICGtesting.com
LVHW041038231023
761874LV00006B/206

9 780820 365336